MW00834844

Islands and Cultures

Islands and Cultures

How Pacific Islands Provide Paths toward Sustainability

KAMANAMAIKALANI BEAMER
TE MAIRE TAU
PETER M. VITOUSEK

With
Atholl Anderson
Oliver A. Chadwick
T. Kaeo Duarte
Sonia Haoa
Patrick V. Kirch
Natalie Kurashima
Thegn N. Ladefoged
Noa K. Lincoln
Pamela A. Matson
Christopher M. Stevenson
Mehana Blaich Vaughan
Kawika B. Winter

Yale UNIVERSITY PRESS

New Haven and London

Published with assistance from the Ishiyama Family Foundation.

Published with assistance from the foundation established in memory of Philip Hamilton McMillan of the Class of 1894, Yale College.

Yale University Press books may be purchased in quantity for educational, business, or promotional use. For information, please e-mail sales.press@yale.edu (U.S. office) or sales@yaleup.co.uk (U.K. office).

Set in Minion type by IDS Infotech, Ltd.

Library of Congress Control Number: 2021953513
ISBN 978-0-300-25300-9 (hardcover)
ISBN 978-0-300-25301-6 (paper)

A catalogue record for this book is available from the British Library.

*We dedicate this book to Neil J. Kahoʻokele Hannahs,
who brought us together through the First Nations'
Futures Program and whose dedication to Indigenous
advancement across the Pacific inspires us*

Kimihia te pūkenga wai e kotahi ai te mātauranga Pākehā me te mātauranga ō ngā iwi ō Te Moana Nui a Kiwa. He arahou kei reira mā tātou mā te tangata, e ora ai Te Aitanga a Papatu-anuku.

Search for the confluence where the waters of Western knowledge and Pacific indigenous knowledge meet. Humanity's future path is there, a path by which our Mother the Earth and all of her descendants may yet thrive.

—JUSTICE SIR JOE WILLIAMS, New Zealand Supreme Court

Contents

Acknowledgments ix

A Note on Language xi

Introduction 1

Part I: Background

ONE. Who Are the Polynesians and What Is Polynesia? 11

TWO. Polynesian Islands as Model Social-Environmental
Systems 22

Part II: Narratives of Islands and Societies

THREE. Hawai'i 35

FOUR. Rapa Nui (Easter Island) Rock Gardens 76

FIVE. Tikopia: A 3,000-Year Journey toward Sustainability 94

SIX. Mahinga kai nō Tonganui (New Zealand): Making a
Living in South Polynesia, 1250–1800 111

Part III: Comparisons and Syntheses

SEVEN. The Hidden *Pā* of Knowledge and the Mind
of Māori 141

EIGHT. Similarities and Differences in Island Social-
Environmental Systems 173

NINE. Sustainability in Polynesian Island Societies 185

Glossary of Selected Terms 201
Selected References and Suggestions for
Further Reading 209
List of Contributors 221
Index 223

Acknowledgments

We thank Margaret Ishiyama Raffin and the Ishiyama Family Foundation for their support, including a production subvention; S. C. Hotchkiss for her helpful comments on the first and the last three chapters; and Liana Matson Vitousek for preparing most of the maps and figures. We also thank The Woods Institute for the Environment at Stanford University for hosting the First Nations' Futures Institute, which brought us together. And we thank Jean Thomson Black and Mary Pasti of Yale University Press for their unflagging support for this book.

Of the lead authors, Kamanamaikalani Beamer is Native Hawaiian and is the Dana Naone Hall Endowed Chair and a professor at the Center for Hawaiian Studies at the University of Hawaiʻi at Mānoa, with a joint appointment at the Richardson School of Law and the Hawaiʻinuiākea School of Hawaiian Knowledge. Te Maire Tau is Māori and an associate professor and director of the Ngāi Tahu Research Centre at the University of Canterbury, Christchurch, New Zealand. Peter Vitousek is not Polynesian but was born and raised in Hawaiʻi; he is a professor of biology at Stanford University. All three have collaborated for a number of years in the First Nations' Futures Program, an alliance of Native Hawaiian, New Zealand Māori, and Alaska Native organizations that supports an annual institute at Stanford University. We thank the program and are excited to extend our collaboration to this volume.

A Note on Language

All Polynesian languages are closely related and mutually understandable. Polynesian languages were not written languages for most of their history, although they are now vibrant written as well as spoken languages. We use Polynesian words throughout this book, providing the closest English translations we can manage. Some words have no English equivalent. Since we are publishing this book in English, we also use English words and supply Polynesian words in a glossary.

In Polynesian words we use diacritical marks to show sounds without English equivalents and as a guide to pronunciation. The marks we use are the glottal stop (ʻ) and the macron (ˉ). The glottal stop, called an ʻokina in Hawaiian, is pronounced like the pause in the English expression "uh-oh." The macron, called kahakō in Hawaiian and tohutō in Māori, is placed above a vowel to indicate a long vowel sound, as in "cape." For comparison, "cap" has a short vowel sound.

Islands and Cultures

Introduction

Kamanamaikalani Beamer, Te Maire Tau,
and Peter M. Vitousek

Today there is little doubt of the remarkable skill, courage, and vision of our early ancestors who voyaged across the Pacific Ocean. Centuries prior to Colombus's arrival in the Americas, master navigators of the Pacific changed the world when they discovered tiny distant islands, thereby expanding oceanic culture, plants, and agricultural techniques across an immense part of the globe. The captains and wayfinders of Pacific voyaging canoes charted their courses to our island homes—among the most isolated lands in the world—and back again to their original homes using their mastery of stars, winds, and waves. They could predict the movement of stars and other bodies in the heavens to navigate a course. They developed methods to utilize wind and swell directions to maintain the course. And they possessed an intimate understanding of marine species, which allowed them to approximate location and distance from landfall while traversing open water. We were navigators, we were explorers, we were oceanic peoples who settled, dwelt in, and acquired a similar intimacy with the natural world of our new island homes. We developed complex social systems and some large agricultural systems that became almost entirely dependent on our island locations. Our relationships with our sea and our islands shaped a substantial part of what we consider our culture today.

Do properties of a place or landscape that support a particular human society influence features of that society? That is the question addressed in this book. The question has a long and contentious history, in large part because affirmative answers to the question have been used to justify the ugly realities of colonialism and the maintenance of the status quo resulting from colonialism. The label "environmental determinism" can be sufficient to dismiss analyses that attribute those realities to the places where they arose. However, we do not know any Indigenous individuals who live within their culture who would say that the land, and, more broadly, the environment, does *not* influence society in important ways. Moreover, we, including all the authors collectively, know many Indigenous islanders who say that the influence of the environment on features of their society was paramount in forming an Indigenous identity. Perhaps, then, it is time to interrogate the widespread dismissal of environmental influence on human societies, recognize that there are interactions and feedbacks between the land and human societies, and accept that these relationships occur within integrated social-environmental systems.

A related debate, and a staple of college dormitory bull sessions, is to dissect the importance of nature versus nurture in human activities. Most scholars come to recognize that engaging in that debate is unproductive; nature and nurture interact in such deeply entangled ways that assigning a fractional contribution of each to many human behaviors has no value. Similarly, landscapes—here, specific islands—are influenced by both biophysical features of the land and features of the human societies that occupy the land. The biophysical features of the land influence local human societies just as human societies influence the biophysical features of the land. Social and biophysical processes interact deeply and complexly to shape landscapes and to shape each other, so untangling the fractional contributions of each to any particular landscape is challenging (and ultimately pointless). The importance of the interactions is recognized in many modern analyses that focus on social-environmental systems or coupled human and natural systems.

Allowing for interaction between social and environmental systems seems obvious, but acceptance of that way of thinking about landscapes has been slow and remains incomplete. Ordinary citizens may reject the possible strength of the influence of the environment on societies, having an understandable concern about environmental determinism and its toxic legacy. But many ecologists also spend productive careers studying human impacts on ecosystems while not paying attention to reciprocal effects of ecosystems on humans. More perniciously, those espousing the ideology of wilderness assume that there are places that are not and should not be shaped by human activity. In fact, wherever people have been, they have influenced the land (and, we add, have been influenced by the land). People have been almost everywhere on earth. Many of the features of so-called wilderness that visitors find appealing are a consequence of the interactions between people (in the first instance, Indigenous societies) and ecosystems. All humans modify the land and always have done so—and all land has features that constrain or enable modifications that will support human well-being or will not.

In this book, we explore relationships among features of the land and characteristics of oceanic societies in the era before globalization. The Pacific island societies we write about offer an extraordinary opportunity to understand how human societies and the land interact in the context of integrated social-environmental systems. What many people today term the Polynesian people journeyed across much of the Pacific on voyages of discovery and colonization between 3,000 and 800 years ago. In their voyaging, Polynesians discovered many previously uninhabited islands in the great Pacific triangle bounded by Hawai'i in the north, Rapa Nui (Easter Island) in the southeast, and Aotearoa (New Zealand) in the southwest. The islands they discovered were varied: some were large, some small; some had fertile soil, some infertile soil; some derived from oceanic and continental volcanism, from coral, from the drifting remnants of continents. Collectively the islands they discovered represented the entire spectrum of ecological zones that exist on earth. They included, for example, coral atolls like the Tuamotus, which are poor in terrestrial but rich in marine resources; diverse volcanic high islands like Hawai'i, which has some fertile soils and well-watered valleys; small and infertile volcanic islands like Rapa Nui (1 percent the size of Hawai'i); and the large, temperate, glacier-supporting subcontinental islands of Aotearoa.

Our ancestors carried most of the important components of their material culture with them as they traveled, though not always on their initial voyages or at the same time. Besides their crops, domestic animals, and other culturally important plants and animals, they carried ancestral ideas of how these plants and animals could be used to increase the productivity of landscapes, along with technologies and ideas of a social organization that facilitated the growth and sustainable use of these resources. Many of the islands they discovered would not support the systems they had in mind or even the growth of some or all of their transported crops, so they had to adapt and adjust their systems to the properties of their islands. Adaptation and adjustment to features of particular islands, and reciprocal changes to islands, represent the focus of this volume.

While it may be so obvious as to pass without notice, we believe it is important to emphasize that our ancestors' societies were, and remain, island societies. Islands have long been models that have facilitated an understanding of the world. Perhaps the clearest example to date is the study of evolution and the formation of new species, which is most comprehensible on islands; it is no coincidence that after visiting the Galápagos Islands, Charles Darwin wrote, in *The Voyage of the Beagle,* first published in 1839, that there "both in space and time, we seem to be brought somewhat near to that great fact—that mystery of mysteries—the first appearance of new beings on this earth." Darwin's genius lay in moving from seeming "to be brought somewhat near" to coming up with a coherent theory of evolution by natural selection. His observations on the Galápagos Islands were key to his insights, and islands have remained central to our ability to understand evolution.

Equally, islands can, as unique models, aid in understanding the complexities of social-environmental and coupled human and natural systems. The scale of islands and their terrestrial boundedness, the common origins of Polynesian societies, their historically recent discovery, and the geological consistency of many islands—all of these factors make Pacific islands models for understanding how societies form and develop. Changes to the islands occurred rapidly, so studying islands can also illuminate how societies can make a transition toward sustainability.

The development of the productive systems of societies on different islands can be usefully compared to the evolutionary process of adaptive radiation. Although analogies between biological and cultural evolution can be misleading, this one seems apt. Adaptive radiation is an important evolutionary process in which lineages of organisms diversify rapidly from an ancestral species, resulting in a multitude of new forms, particularly when a change in the environment makes new resources available, creates new opportunities or challenges, or opens new environmental niches. Adaptive radiation can be considered opportunity-driven speciation, because new species develop over time when there is an opportunity for a different form to succeed. In a similar way, Polynesian societies made use of the opportunities as well as constraints of new islands to develop a wide range of new social-environmental systems. Sometimes they developed diverse types of social-environmental systems within a single island or archipelago, when variation in features of the land facilitated their development of diversity. This development and diversification of social-environmental systems can be considered opportunity-driven in that it depended on innovations developed by Polynesians that were often outside the range of their ancestors' experiences.

Throughout this volume, we consider how Polynesian societies were influenced by the lands they discovered and how they in turn influenced those lands. We pay particular attention to innovations that facilitated the development of highly populous and socially and culturally complex societies on very different islands and to innovations that supported a transition to sustainable ways of living on some of those islands. Patrick Kirch opened many of these lines of inquiry in his analysis "Three Islands and an Archipelago" (2007), and we build upon many of his insights here. We include some islands that Kirch did not—notably Rapa Nui and Aotearoa—and we privilege scholarship by Indigenous Polynesians where it is available. (Sources mentioned in the text are included in the list with the suggestions for further reading.) Hawai'i and Aotearoa in particular support strong communities of Polynesian scholars, and the wealth of knowledge and insights they bring to these analyses is new, powerful, and likely to spread to other regions of the Pacific in coming decades. We hope that this volume will become one of the catalysts for that spread.

This book is organized in three sections. In the first, we introduce the volume, describe who Polynesians are, how we originated, and why Polynesian societies are particularly useful for this analysis (even in comparison to other Pacific island societies), and develop the concept of social-environmental systems and Polynesian islands as model systems for understanding their development and dynamics.

The second section includes brief narrative histories of several Polynesian islands or archipelagoes. Here, in most cases, young Polynesian scholars are writing about the history of their own societies. The coverage of Polynesian societies is not encyclopedic; the selected societies are illustrative of the major points of the volume, and interested young scholars from those societies are willing to do the analysis. The chapters in this section are heterogeneous because the interests and backgrounds of their authors are heterogeneous. There are cultural narratives as well as archaeological summaries, with the latter guided by the very different traditions of American versus European academic archaeology (including in those written by Indigenous archaeologists). All of the chapters address our core question of how islands and societies interact, although at times they do so in very different ways and from very different perspectives. The chapter on Tikopia, which is crucially important for any discussion of a transition to sustainability in Polynesia (or anywhere else) and for which we know of no Indigenous scholars, was written by Patrick Kirch based on his extensive experience there and elsewhere in Polynesia.

The third section of the book builds on the background in the first section and the historical narratives of societies in the second section to provide a rich analysis of human-land interactions in Polynesian societies. Important considerations there are the ways that some Polynesian societies innovated the most explicitly sustainable social-environmental systems anywhere, and we ask whether their pathways to sustainability might contribute to modern societies' efforts to address similar challenges. We do not privilege a particular worldview, but we do privilege Indigenous societies' choices of the tools they find useful for understanding the world, and we celebrate the realization of those choices in Polynesia and the value of their choices for all societies.

I
Background

1

Who Are the Polynesians and What Is Polynesia?

Kamanamaikalani Beamer, Peter M. Vitousek,
and Te Maire Tau

*H*e wa'a he moku, he moku he wa'a, "The canoe is an island, the island is a canoe." If there is any coherent way of discussing the origins of the people anthropologists have come to know as Polynesians, it is by acknowledging that our genealogies, stories, and knowledge base are tied to our relationships with the sea. Our intimate understandings of the natural systems of the sea are reflected in the various oceanic manifestations of the *akua* (god) Kanaloa. As we navigated across Kanaloa's vast domain and pulled islands out of the sea, we also carried with us names such as Hava'iki/Hawai'i/Savai'i, Kona/Tonga, Hāmoa /Sāmoa, Ko'olau/Tokelau, and others that appear across our "sea of islands" (the noted scholar Epeli Hau'ofa's phrase). Is the ocean a boundary or a bridge? For Polynesians, the peoples of the canoe, our ocean connects us, it feeds us, it is our home. Another character whose deeds are known across the Pacific is

Maui. We all know how he snared the sun and slowed it down to extend daylight, or how he fetched the secrets of fire for humankind, or how his descendants voyaged to places such as Aotearoa (New Zealand), whose South Island carries the name *Te Waka ō Māui* (the canoe of Maui). Whether the islands and cultures of Oceania appear to be a group of tiny islands in a vast sea or a vast sea full of islands depends entirely on frame of reference and relationship to the ocean.

The first Europeans to encounter multiple Polynesian societies—notably the English captain James Cook and his crew—were surprised to encounter similar peoples separated by many thousands of kilometers of open ocean. On visiting Rapa Nui (Easter Island) after spending time in Tahiti and Aotearoa, Cook wrote, in *A Voyage Towards the South Pole and Round the World* (1777), that "in color, features, and language, they [the local islanders] bear such an affinity to the people of the more western isles, that no one will doubt they have had the same origin. It is extraordinary that the same nation should have spread themselves over all the isles in this vast ocean, from New Zealand to this island, which is almost one-fourth part of the circumference of the globe." Cook and his contemporaries thus began a continuing series of speculations about the extraordinary history of Polynesians. More remains to be understood about the origins of the Polynesian peoples and cultures, but analyses of the people and the plants and animals they transported, detailed studies of languages, and the success of long-distance voyaging by modern Polynesian navigators have provided answers to many of the questions that concerned Cook and his contemporaries. Although there remain areas of uncertainty and active areas of research on Polynesian origins, the focus here is on a core of information that scholars of Pacific history widely agree on. Throughout this book, we seek to navigate between worldviews. We do not privilege any worldview, but we do privilege Indigenous societies' ability to choose the tools they find useful for understanding the world, and we celebrate the realization of those choices in Polynesia and the value of this navigation for all societies.

The story of Polynesian origins begins with the migration of groups of people into Southeast Asia and what is now Australia many tens of thousands of years ago. These people must have moved rapidly across Asia when humans migrated out of Africa. This wave of migration occurred when sea levels were substantially lower than at present, and much of what is now Island Southeast Asia was connected to the Asian continent. Sea levels rose as continental glaciers melted in the present interglacial epoch, so the traversed land is now under the sea. These groups of people did not confine themselves to land journeys; they must have made their way across several channels between islands that are deep enough that they have remained underwater for millions of years. The most famous of these long-standing ocean barriers is what academic scholars call Wallace's Line, which runs between Bali and Lombok. Bali was connected to Asia through what are now Java and Sumatra in glacial times when sea levels were low, and Lombok was not connected to Asia by land. Wallace's Line marks a geographic separation between groups of organisms that could not cross the ocean barriers between what we may call Asia and Australia. Unlike many animals, people were not stopped by straits where seawater remained; they crossed land and ocean to New Guinea and to Australia (which were then connected) and out even farther to the extreme eastern edge of the Solomon Islands. Their ocean crossings were between lands that were intervisible at least some of the time. This early migration continued in waves; multiple groups of people traveled to Asia over tens of thousands of years. As time passed, the groups of migrants diversified in culture and language; they are the progenitors of Aboriginal Australians and the people of the New Guinea Highlands, among others.

The story of Polynesian origins continued with the migrations of a second group of people from continental Asia into Island Southeast Asia. These people migrated from Taiwan and the Philippines to what are now Indonesia and New Guinea and the surrounding islands. This group migrated just a few thousand years ago, when sea levels were similar to those today, so they had to cross more and longer expanses of ocean than the previous group did. They spoke a very different language, too; their language gave rise to what is now termed the Austronesian language family. There is evidence that they remained ocean-oriented once they reached New Guinea; about 50 of the 800 languages now spoken in Papua New Guinea belong to the Austronesian language family, and all the speakers are from the coast and offshore islands. The two groups of people exchanged genetic information, as people do. At some point, perhaps 3,000 years ago, a blended group speaking an Austronesian language made the huge leap from the Solomon Islands—still considered Near Oceania because of the islands' proximity to Asia—to the more remote archipelagoes of Fiji, Samoa, and Tonga. Reaching Remote Oceania required a departure to an unseen destination and a journey across hundreds of kilometers of ocean. When or shortly after these progenitors of the Polynesian people made their leap, their canoes carried a suite of plants and animals that were the basis not only of their diet and their productive systems but also of their notions of identity and morality.

Once these voyagers reached Fiji, Samoa, and Tonga at the edge of Remote Oceania, they and their descendants probably remained there for many generations, developing a distinctive way of life: a culture. During this time, the fusion of the earlier migrants and the later ones continued; by then it would have made sense to speak of a unified Polynesian people. This unity resulted from the fusion of what had been two distinct groups of people; it was not a unity born of independent origins but a real unity nonetheless. The early Polynesians had a distinctive language within the Austronesian language family; they had a distinct set of plants and animals that they managed for food and other uses; and they had a distinct and defined clan-based social organization.

At some point, groups began migrating again, this time as Polynesians, heading out from Fiji, Samoa, and Tonga. The nature of their migrations was long debated, but we now believe that they embarked on deliberate voyages of discovery and colonization. Polynesian and other Pacific navigators could use celestial observations to fix the latitude of their home islands, then take advantage of occasional reversals in the prevailing southeast trade winds, the dominant winds of the southern hemisphere tropics, to launch voyages to the east. Multiple cues told them when they were close to an island and in which direction an island lay, including the reflections of waves off islands, cloud patterns, and the flight of land-nesting seabirds at sunrise and sunset. Any island they found would be uninhabited, as all islands of Remote Oceania were until Polynesians found them, and they could use plants and animals from home to establish a new society. If they failed to find an island and if food or water was becoming short, they could sail to the latitude of their home island and then rapidly sail back to it downwind. Their voyages were dangerous, no doubt, but they were not desperate journeys to discover new homes or die in the attempt. The extraordinary voyages by the Polynesian Voyaging Society in the *Hōkūleʻa* and other recently built double-hulled sailing canoes demonstrate both the seaworthiness of traditional vessels and the value of traditional way-finding techniques.

Many islands and archipelagoes lie to the east of Fiji, Samoa, and Tonga in the southeast trade wind belt, and Polynesian voyagers found them all. Later, probably after all the habitable southern hemisphere tropical islands had been discovered and colonized, they voyaged more widely, perhaps following the paths of what they knew to be migratory birds, like the golden plover and the shearwater, to the Hawaiian Archipelago and Aotearoa. These later voyages were more challenging; for example, getting to Hawai'i from the southern Pacific required traversing the doldrums (the Intertropical Convergence Zone), where winds are shifting and unreliable, as well as sailing with and against both the southeast and the northeast trade winds. Still, modern navigators from the Polynesian Voyaging Society have managed the trips successfully, again using only traditional sailing canoes and traditional way-finding techniques.

The Polynesian discovery and colonization of the Pacific was rapid. It is tempting to think of Polynesians finding an archipelago—say, the islands of Hiva (Marquesas Islands)—establishing a society there, and then, when there was no more land to develop, setting off on voyages of discovery and ultimately landing in the Hawaiian Islands. If that view of history were accurate, features of the Polynesian society that had adapted to the Marquesas Islands would be expected to influence Polynesian societies in Hawai'i. Rather, we now believe that Polynesian voyagers during their great age of discovery were committed to discovery; upon finding the islands of Hiva, some people would remain and establish a society, and others would rapidly (within a generation or two) move on to further discoveries. That age of discovery did not persist. Oral traditions show that there was two-way voyaging between Hawai'i and the rest of Polynesia for a few centuries after Hawai'i was discovered, but those long-distance voyages ceased several centuries before European contact.

The extent to which Polynesian voyagers traversed the globe has been the subject of scientific debate for generations.

We now believe that voyagers probably made it as far as the coasts of the Americas, a view supported by both anthropological and genetic evidence of Polynesian exchange with the Indigenous inhabitants of present-day Colombia. One line of evidence is the distribution of the important food plant sweet potato, which, like the bottle gourd, is of American origin. Most of the other crops that Polynesians distributed across the Pacific are Asian or Papuan in origin. Even the Polynesian word for sweet potato shows a connection with the people of South America. The name *kumara* (in Hawaiian, *'uala*) is similar to the one used by Indigenous peoples of the Americas. Also, genetic material derived from Native people of the Colombian coast is widely distributed through eastern Polynesia. Neither genetic information nor linguistic similarity nor crop plants can determine who sailed where, just that people must have been in contact with each other, but the Polynesians were the greatest sailors and navigators of the era, and it makes sense to us that they were the ones who voyaged to the Americas. Even discounting trips to the Americas, by any scholarly account the explorations by Polynesians are remarkable. They traversed a vast expanse of the globe.

The consequences of their voyages were remarkably different from the consequences of European explorations in the centuries to follow. Let us be clear: colonialism and slavery were not outcomes of these Polynesian explorations. However, given the extent of Polynesian exploration, it may still be useful to compare their voyages with the European voyages of discovery. Spanish fleets were in the Pacific from the 1500s through the early 1800s, carrying on annual trading voyages between Acapulco, Mexico, and Manila, in the Philippines—trips covering a wide expanse of the Pacific Ocean—but their voyages left much of the Pacific unknown to Europeans. Then, in the late 1700s, James Cook—who wrote, in *A Voyage Towards the South*

Pole and Round the World, that he sought to travel "not only farther than any other man has been before me, but as far as I think it possible for man to go"— deliberately sailed into areas of the Pacific of which Europeans knew little, quickly adding most of the major islands of the Pacific to European knowledge. There are many differences between Cook and the Polynesian navigators, not least that Polynesians traveled to places that no human had been before. Cook, in effect, followed them there. Polynesian navigators may nonetheless have recognized in him a kindred voyager.

A further parallel between the voyages of the Polynesian navigators and those of James Cook may be that both were motivated in part by cosmologies that we now consider to be incomplete, even inaccurate. Polynesian navigators sought to sail into the prevailing winds to reach islands that they believed would be associated with bright stars. Every known island had a "zenith star," a star that was directly overhead at a particular time of the year. That observation contributed to Polynesians' knowledge of the latitude of their home island and their ability to return to it. It was not a great stretch to assume that every star—at least, every bright star—was the zenith star for an island. Finding a new island, one that lay under a bright star with no known island associated with it, became a matter of sailing far enough into the prevailing winds to reach that island. There were enough islands in the South Pacific that such voyages often were successful; if a voyage failed to reach a new island, the navigator could sail downwind for home in the latitude of the home island without any necessary challenge to that belief system: after all, the island might have been just a little farther away.

James Cook was charged with finding the Great Southern Continent, a land mass that European geographers of his time believed had to exist in the temperate South Pacific. Because the known continents occurred disproportionately in the northern hemisphere, they reasoned there must be a large un-known land mass in the southern hemisphere to balance the distribution of land between the hemispheres.

We now consider both lines of reasoning to be flawed; stars are not associated with islands except in human minds after the fact of discovery, and land masses need not be balanced between hemispheres (and indeed they are not balanced). Nevertheless, both cosmologies motivated explorations that led to real discoveries.

Polynesia as a geographical location is the area that was discovered and occupied by Polynesian people. There is some blurring of the distinctiveness of Polynesian people in some areas at the margin of their lands, so there is some ambiguity in determining Polynesia's boundaries. Nevertheless, it is gen-erally agreed that the location of Polynesia is defined by a tri-angle with apices in the Hawaiian Islands, in Aotearoa, and in Rapa Nui, with some Polynesian societies and so some Polyne-sian lands occurring to the west of this triangle (figure 1.1). The Polynesian Triangle itself occupies an ocean area of about 50 million square kilometers, about five times the land area of the United States (including Alaska). That is the scale and scope of the Polynesian peoples' voyages of discovery. Within that 50 million square kilometers of ocean, only a little over 300,000 square kilometers is land—and of that land, nearly 90 percent is in Aotearoa and half of the remainder in Hawai'i. The lands of Polynesia are among the areas on the earth that have been most recently occupied by humans; only Iceland and Greenland are comparable. Nor did any of the Polynesian islands have human populations before the arrival of Polynesians.

Europeans who encountered Pacific societies divided them into three large groupings that are still used today—Polynesians, Micronesians, and Melanesians—thereby establishing a classification that Pacific islanders of that time would not have

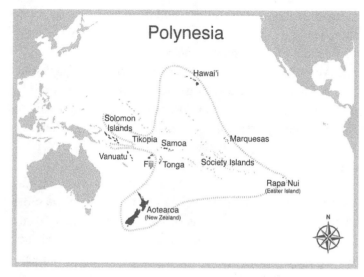

Figure 1.1. The Polynesian Triangle, showing the distribution of
Polynesian societies in the Pacific Ocean and the locations of
Aotearoa, Rapa Nui, Hawai'i, and Tikopia. The first three of
these are at the apices of the Polynesian triangle.

recognized. Nor is it well regarded by either scholars or Pacific
islanders today. Of these three groups, only Polynesians represent
a natural grouping based on genetics, language, and culture—
and as we saw, the unity of Polynesians is a matter of fusion
rather than independent origins. So-called Micronesians are a
blend of the same founding groups as Polynesians (early and
late migrants to Island Southeast Asia), but they descend from
at least three separate colonizations of Remote Oceania, reached
from three different starting points. So-called Melanesians also
descend from multiple groups of (mostly early) migrants;
moreover, they have been present in Island Southeast Asia
for so long that it is difficult to trace their cultural history in
interaction with the islands they dwell on. In an analogy to

evolutionary biology, we could say that Polynesians represent a monophyletic group—a group that descended from common ancestors who shared distinct genes, language, and culture—while both so-called Micronesians and Melanesians are polyphyletic, having descended from multiple independent groups of ancestors. Polynesian societies thus illustrate more clearly than the others how human societies and cultures change in the course of human adjustment to different lands. The other societies may be equally creative and interesting in the ways they adjusted to conditions on their new island homes, but the Polynesian story is straightforward and instructive, as we will see.

2

Polynesian Islands as Model Social-Environmental Systems

Peter M. Vitousek and Kawika B. Winter

T he islands discovered by Polynesian navigators were among the last places on earth to be reached by humans, so it is relatively straightforward to see how the new residents transitioned from living in natural systems dominated by biophysical features to developing social-environmental systems with both biophysical and social controls. Polynesian discoverers brought the essential components of their culture and economy with them in their voyaging canoes—multiple food and other crops, domestic animals, and, inevitably but inadvertently, some of the plants and animals that accompany people everywhere and that are termed weeds and pests. Besides the components of their culture and economy, they also brought previously tested strategies for integrating those components into a system of production, as well as philosophies on how human society could be regulated to interact positively with a system of production.

Upon arrival, Polynesians began to engineer both landscapes and seascapes to make use of the many features of the ecosystems that facilitate an abundance of resources for human societies. Some of the changes were no doubt inadvertent; for example, rats that arrived on the canoes spread into the forests and, through seed predation and in other ways, shifted the composition and character of entire forests, which probably contributed to the extinction of many plants and animals. However, some of the changes in landscape and seascape were initial steps in the voyagers' attempts to make a newly discovered island more familiar by tapping into strategies and philosophies that they brought with them.

Highly productive areas such as riparian zones and estuaries were stabilized and expanded to increase food production. Alluvial plains and other gently sloping lands were terraced, and streams were diverted to support wetland agroecosystems—as in the lands the discoverers traveled from. These systems were designed both to support the production of complex carbohydrates (taro) and to increase the availability of protein by expanding habitat for native fish and waterfowl.

In steeper areas and in areas too far from streams to be irrigated, forests were either maintained in an augmented state (e.g., by changing the species composition to increase food production) or cut and burned in cycles of shifting cultivation. Shifting cultivation contributed to an erosional pattern that favored the delivery of topsoil and its nutrients to cultivated valleys.

The discoverers' engineering and management activities permanently altered the hydrology and land-sea interactions of these islands. In nearshore environments, large marine predators were targeted and managed to favor the populations of herbivorous marine fauna, which are systematically more productive than carnivores in providing protein for human consumption. While the extent to which some of these individual aspects of system-level management were undertaken deliberately to improve human well-being is debatable, the manner in which the changes worked together at a landscape and seascape level to stabilize and to increase food production and other ecosystem services is clear.

Crucially, biophysical features of some smaller islands constrained the capacity for implementing the practices that people might have had in mind on arrival, and biophysical features of the fully temperate islands of Aotearoa (New Zealand) and nearby islands were incompatible with the agricultural systems that Polynesian voyagers brought with them during their diaspora. Both small and temperate islands effectively limited the options for system-level engineering and design that their ancestors had developed. The new situation was not conducive for the conversion of a large fraction of the island's surface (and the surrounding ocean) using the templates for production systems that the Polynesian discoverers carried in their toolkits. The climate of much of Aotearoa, for example, did not allow for the growth of any Polynesian food crops over most of the land during the winter season—and the summer season was too short south of the Banks Peninsula (near Christchurch) on Te Wai Pounamu (the South Island) for any transported Polynesian crops to grow to maturity at all. Given such constraints, the Polynesian discoverers had to adjust their production systems to work in their new environment. At this point, we are dealing with social-environmental systems—not simply natural systems altered by human intervention, and not social systems imposed on a new land, but rather interactions of social and natural systems that could continue to develop in new ways and on their own paths.

The transition to social-environmental systems did not require the presence of important environmental constraints like those imposed by the seasonality of Aotearoa. In time, Polynesian societies discovered opportunities that their new islands provided that may not have been available in their homelands—and they innovated new production systems that took advantage of the new opportunities. Such innovations represent interactions of social and environmental systems that could develop into new social-environmental systems.

One of the many ways to examine the development of social-environmental systems over time is through the challenges their developers faced in regard to sustainability and the success they had in overcoming those challenges. Differing templates of land management—such as differing systems of intensive food production—have differing degrees of malleability in terms of sustainably fitting into a landscape. Some templates that are inflexibly imposed on landscapes rapidly degrade the resource base that supports them. In the long term, this degradation threatens the very existence of these systems of production. The development of social-environmental systems like the ones implemented by many modern societies emphasize intensive food production without balanced consideration for the longer-term sustainability of that production or the other values of that land; consequently, they often carry within themselves the seeds of their own destruction. Polynesian societies took different approaches to systems management, based in large part on a worldview that regarded land and living organisms as kin as well as resources.

A central point of this book is that the development and dynamics of social-environmental systems are not only relatively clear on Polynesian islands, but they are clearer on Polynesian islands than anywhere else in the world. Polynesian islands are remarkable models for understanding how social-ecological systems can arise and develop and thus, we suggest, models for understanding the long-term sustainability of human societies. The concept of model systems is widely used in biology, where it means something more than "examples." Rather, model systems are systems that make a general process or property accessible to understanding. Here is a case in point. In biology, research on the conduction of nerve impulses originally focused on the giant axons (connections between nerve cells) of the squid genus *Loligo;* these axons are more than a thousand times larger in diameter than most vertebrate nerve axons and could be studied directly with the electrodes available in the 1960s and 1970s. It was not the squid per se that was of interest but nerve conduction in general, using the squid as a model system to understand the process.

A more recent case is the use of the nematode *Caenorhabditis elegans* as a model system. *C. elegans* is widely used for studies of the molecular biology of how organisms develop because it is an integrated multicellular organism and yet it is remarkably simple. It has specialized "muscles," digestive tissue, a nervous system, and gametes; it undergoes reproduction and development and aging. At the same time, *C. elegans* is small (about 1 millimeter long at maturity), has a short generation time, and is readily grown in culture. Physically, it is transparent, so the movement and fate of individual cells and their daughters can be followed directly. Finally, an adult *C. elegans* is made up of only 959 non-reproductive cells, whose formation and movements can be followed directly, manipulated experimentally, and understood on the basis of both genetics and biochemistry.

The use of *C. elegans* as a model organism was not based on the expectation that its developmental program would be just like that of other organisms; the greater complexity of most multicellular animals ensures otherwise. Rather, the expectation (now abundantly realized) was that the simplicity of the *C. elegans* system would allow many of the most fundamental mechanisms involved in development to be understood—and that the understanding gained by studying *C. elegans* would be useful in the analysis of more complex organisms. In this sense, *C. elegans* was selected as a model system because it represented a useful compromise between complexity and tractability. Other widely used model systems in physiology and molecular biology include fruit flies, the small mustard *Arabidopsis thaliana,* the bacterium *Escherichia coli,* and the ubiquitous laboratory rats and mice.

Islands have long been used as model systems for a wide range of investigations—most notably evolution and the formation of new species. Islands have been central to the study of speciation (the formation of new species) at least since Darwin, after visiting the Galápagos Islands, wrote in *The Voyage of the Beagle* of being "near, both in space and time," to "the first appearance of new beings on this earth." It is not just speciation that has been studied most effectively on islands; many concepts in evolution—including adaptive radiation, described earlier—were first or best developed in studies carried out on oceanic islands. Today, islands remain an extraordinary development and testing ground for many aspects of understanding evolution.

Studies of terrestrial ecosystems have also made productive use of islands as models. Islands have well-defined boundaries, making it possible to study them as whole systems. Also, the underlying rock of most remote oceanic high islands—those that reach well above sea level—is basalt, with a relatively consistent composition in both space and time, and the underlying rock of all atolls is coral. On high islands, rainfall varies in a highly organized and predictable pattern as a function of topography and exposure to prevailing winds, and the age of soils varies similarly as a function of the eruptive history of volcanoes (which is characterized very well on many islands) and the geological age of the islands (similarly characterized well). These features and others have made many aspects of soil development and climate-ecosystem interactions more amenable to understanding on islands than anywhere else. Additionally, some geological features of oceanic islands built from basalt make it possible to identify and understand the sources of nutrients that support soil fertility in a more straightforward way than is possible elsewhere. The combination of tractability and these special features has facilitated discovery of the importance of long-distance transport of dust from arid areas to the maintenance of plant productivity in all rain forests on old soils everywhere on earth; this is one example among many that illustrates how islands facilitate understanding of how ecosystems work.

Here we show that oceanic islands—and especially Polynesian islands—also are useful models for understanding how humans and human societies interact with land. Specifically, we can study the development and dynamics of social-ecological systems. The evolutionary concept of adaptive radiation, again, provides a starting point. The Polynesians are a well-defined and coherent lineage of people and a culture who voyaged to many new islands that offered new constraints and opportunities; the development and dynamics of their new societies on new islands are interesting and useful for understanding social-environmental systems for several reasons, some already suggested; others, logical expansions of those reasons.

1. Both the society of the Polynesians who discovered new islands and the features of the islands themselves are better defined and characterized than are most other societies and lands. Consequently, the interaction of culture and land is more accessible to understanding for Polynesian islands than elsewhere.

2. Polynesian islands are among the most recent places anywhere on earth to be discovered by humans and are among the last places on earth to be converted from ecosystems into social-ecological systems. Consequently, Polynesian societies are young by global standards, and their history is more accessible through multiple forms of analysis (including oral history) than is the case in most places.

3. Island societies are isolated. Their isolation is far from complete—Polynesian navigators of their age of discovery, like Polynesians today, considered the ocean to be a connection between islands as well as something that divided them. However, it remains generally true that island societies are less driven by interactions with neighboring societies than are continental societies, whose neighbors are right next door, so internal dynamics are relatively more important than external dynamics on islands versus continents.

4. Polynesian societies were and are innovative and dynamic. Before contact with the rest of the world, they developed remarkable new systems of production. After European contact, Polynesian societies adopted, adapted, and incorporated elements of technology and social organization from elsewhere to their cultures and societies. Their creativity and innovation, starting from a relatively consistent founding culture, make Polynesian societies a useful model for understanding what humanity is capable of achieving.

5. Polynesian societies are living societies. Understanding their history and dynamics is not a

matter of exhuming the features of an extinct
society; rather, Polynesian historians and other
scholars are intrigued by and central to understanding how their individual societies contribute
to understanding human societies in general.

Gaining a more nuanced understanding of changes in
social-environmental systems through time is highly relevant
in the twenty-first century. Each stable or transitional condition
along the path from prehuman ecosystems to human-influenced
social-environmental systems, as well as those states managed
by different dominant cultures or resulting from changes in
practices within a culture, affected the structure and dynamics
of social-environmental systems. We now have the knowledge
and history to analyze how these different systems functioned
and can contribute to the creation of viable models of sustainability in the era of global change.

Talking about a model system is not a Polynesian way to
view Polynesian society; rather, it represents the imposition of
an academic framework on Indigenous epistemologies. However, the question of how human-land interactions developed
can be posed in different ways. Our Hawaiian colleague Neil J.
Kaho'okele Hannahs asks, "When and how did Hawaiians become Hawaiian?" His answer to "when" is that they became
Hawaiian when their interactions with the land of Hawai'i dif-
ferentiated them from their ancestors who had traveled the
Pacific. This differentiation made them into a Hawaiian subset
of Polynesians. The answer to "how" is the central question of
this book. Evaluating islands as models of social-environmental systems is, we believe, a useful way to understand how
Hawaiians became Hawaiian (or Māori became Māori, etc.).
Polynesians see various aspects of nature as manifestations of
their genealogy or the divine. Consequently, those who estab-

lished societies on new islands may have seen their societies as being shaped by deities, as well as by ancestors, rather than by the physical features of the land alone. Indeed, they may not have recognized a distinction between physical features of the land, on the one hand, and ancestors or deities, on the other.

In analyzing the development and dynamics of social-environmental systems, we will focus on food gathering and agriculture. Acquiring food, especially through agriculture, is an important nexus—probably the most important nexus—between society and land. It is obvious how aspects of the land shape what sorts of agriculture are feasible, and agriculture equally obviously affects the dynamics of the land. Polynesians embarked on their voyages of discovery as agriculturists, bringing crops and domestic animals with them, as well as strategies and philosophies for integrating the crops and animals into a system for survival. Because their crops would not grow on some of the islands they discovered, or would not thrive there in the traditional systems for using those crops, they created new forms of high-yielding intensive agriculture and aquaculture in their new lands or developed alternative forms of food gathering and distribution.

Although the greatness of Polynesians as navigators and voyagers is now well appreciated, their greatness as farmers, system engineers, and landscape managers is, we suggest, of a similar magnitude. Our focus is first on understanding how the necessary and widespread innovation of systems of food production across the islands of Polynesia interacted with features of the islands themselves and with the traditional social organization of their founders to drive the development and dynamics of new social-environmental systems. Second, we seek to understand how Polynesian social-environmental systems met the challenges of a transition to sustainability and to explore what Polynesian responses could teach to the modern globalized society that now faces the need for a similar transition.

II
Narratives of Islands and Societies

3
Hawai'i

Noa K. Lincoln, Mehana Blaich Vaughan,
and Natalie Kurashima

Ka Wehena (Opening): Prologue

The development and diversification of integrated social-environmental systems in Hawai'i and elsewhere depended upon adaptation and often involved opportunities and innovations outside the range of ancestral experiences. The pathways of evolution of Pacific island societies have been dependent on a number of environmental variables, some relatively constant over time, such as the structure of the landscape, and some highly variable, such as weather. Some may even be wholly unpredictable and still highly influential, such as the eruption of a volcano. The evolution of societies is also dependent on their people, who, just like their environments, also have some stable common features along with highly variable differences. Given the complex and cumulative nature of culture and its interactions with environment, it can be assumed that no two societies would ever evolve exactly along the same pathways or develop exactly the same features. However, we believe that some broad patterns of variation in social-environmental systems are likely to emerge.

The development of social-environmental systems (a process of cultural evolution) underpins Indigenous resource management. One idea that our ancestors carried with them throughout the Pacific, which has been sustained in Hawai'i, is that plants, animals, and features of the land are kin. Acceptance of this kinship led to a set of practices, norms, and beliefs that emerged to guide our protection of collective well-being by caring for the antecedents of our natural resources. Of all the locations in the world, Hawai'i is one of the most valuable places to observe the natural consequences of caring for people, plants, and the land over time, just as it is among the best places to observe the biological evolution of endemic species. In part this value arises because of the remarkable diversity of landscapes and ecosystems in Hawai'i—a diversity that is highly structured in space. For example, the sequential emergence of the islands creates an age gradient across the archipelago, from young, uncolonized lava flows in the southeast of Hawai'i Island that have yet to feel the generative and sculpting power of the rains and of life to old, depleted soils in the deeply dissected landscapes on Kaua'i's northwestern coast. Groups of people, who originally were very similar, evolved their customs and societies to attune with the diversity of landscapes and seascapes, developing, in the process, distinct communities and practices of interacting with and caring for *'āina,* the inhabited land.

Here, we—three young *kānaka* (Native Hawaiian) scholars—describe the diversity of social-environmental systems across the Hawaiian archipelago by focusing on the places that have shaped each of us and our work. Together, our reflections and research challenge the widespread simplification and homogenization of Hawaiian resource management systems we each encountered in our own growing up and schooling. In weaving our experiences and research together, we seek to make the ingenuity and variation of our ancestors' lives on the land tangible, understandable, and vitally relevant as our people carry this wisdom into present practices and future planning for our children and theirs and theirs.

We will use *kānaka* and *ʻōiwi* to describe ourselves and our people but also at times "Hawaiian," as that is how many sources we cite and most literature refer to our people.

Mehana Blaich Vaughan: During my childhood in the early 1980s, there was little to help me piece together a holistic picture of our ancestors' life on the land. The few books in our public school library hinted at a vibrant, if remote, lifestyle. By grade five I had started working on a plan to establish a settlement somewhere really isolated in Hawaiʻi, where people could live together like our ancestors. Nearly 15 years later, after returning home from college and teaching science and social studies in a Hawaiian-language charter school, I found many more resources were available, even a visual that encapsulated the village life I had envisioned reviving (figure 3.1). This "Ahupuaʻa Poster," showing a traditional Indigenous village, resonated with my experience growing up on the island of Kauaʻi, on the border between the Koʻolau and Haleleʻa *moku,* in areas with plentiful water and streams (see figure 3.2). (*Moku* are traditional land divisions, larger than the *ahupuaʻa,* the traditional land division of the poster.) The poster hung on the wall of my classroom in Honolulu and later rode in the trunk of my Honda when I moved back home to Kauaʻi. There, it traveled from school to school in my car as I taught students about the Hawaiian land-use system that we were helping reinvigorate through stream studies, *loʻi kalo* (taro paddy) restoration work, and community-based projects like those sponsored by the Waipā Foundation. I would point to different sections of the poster to highlight how our ancestors selectively harvested trees from the upland forests, leaving those forests intact to collect water, which then trickled down in

Figure 3.1. "Ahupuaʻa Poster," painted by Marilyn Kahalewai in 1993, depicts an idealized Hawaiian valley society as it would have looked in the years before foreign influence changed the environment and lifestyle of the Hawaiian people. "Makamaluno-honaokalani" by Marilyn Kahalewai is used with permission from Kamehameha Schools.

streams whose use was regulated to maintain the cleanliness of freshwater flows to the sea.

Noa Lincoln: I was born in the *moku* of Kona on the island of Hawai'i, on the opposite end of the archipelago from Kaua'i. The Kona area is leeward of the trade winds and geologically young, with exposed lava rock a dominant feature on the landscape (see figure 3.3). Kona was also home to a major dryland rain-fed agricultural system (a *kānaka* innovation). These particular Hawaiian farming, fishing, and resource-management landscapes and systems were all I interacted with. In fact, I don't think I ever even saw a *lo'i kalo* until I was about 10 years old, in Kīpahulu, Maui. In the sixth grade I distinctly remember seeing the "Ahupua'a Poster" for the first time at my public school and being taught that *ahupua'a* were pie-shaped wedges of land that represented watersheds; they were centered on river valleys and bounded by mountain ridges. Imagine my confusion after spending 99 percent of my life in areas with no rivers and no ridges but that nonetheless were divided into *ahupua'a*. I had learned about the *ahupua'a* of my place for my whole life and how they pertained to our resources and health. To me they looked nothing like what I saw in the poster— nothing like what I was being taught.

Natalie Kurashima: I learned what an *ahupua'a* is from the same poster in my elementary school classroom; at the center of the poster's *ahupua'a* was a stream that ran from the top of a mountain to the sea. There were *kānaka* in traditional clothing who were farming *lo'i kalo*, who had houses to live in and sheds for their canoes, who had fishponds for aquaculture, who were fishing on their canoes. We were told that this represented the *ahupua'a* within which "ancient Hawaiians" lived harmoniously in the past. Perhaps in the same way we engaged in calls and responses with our teacher; using Hawaiian words we didn't understand, we were taught to repeat the concept of

the harmonious *ahupua'a*—a concept that originated in anthropology books about us and our culture and that was subsequently stamped into our impressionable brains each day in
that first-grade classroom.

Over time, I learned, experienced, and connected more
with our living Indigenous Hawaiian concepts and practices
and with our *'āina*, the land where we lived, in which our
worldview is grounded. The *ahupua'a* continues to be codified
in our land systems by our laws and in our government documents; but is it the same *ahupua'a* everywhere, as the laws and
documents suggest? Or should we look and listen more closely
to our communities, to people who have been living for generations in the same *ahupua'a* and collecting a deep, genealogical understanding of their place?

Ke Kumu (Teacher or Source): Introduction

One of our shared mentors, Neil J. Kaho'okele Hannahs, starts
many of his talks by asking, "When did Hawaiians become
Hawaiian?" Our ancestors came from other places, and when
they first stepped off their canoes, they were not Hawaiian. We
agree with our mentor that the place itself was the major influence on the divergence of Hawaiian society. Each group of islands influenced how local society developed. Our ancestors
needed to describe and understand new places and habitats,
resources, plants, and animals. They needed to adapt their
behavior to the local landscape, weather, and biology. Because
of the unique aspects of every place, our ancestors developed
new practices. Over time, the influences between people and
landscape became interactive and circular. Changes made to
the landscape—whether the clearing of a forest or the construction of infrastructure—influenced the way that future generations interacted with the landscape and led their lives. Our

ancestors shaped the land, as the land shaped them. As genealogical connections evolved, places took on new meanings that
encompassed past people and events. As generations passed,
the inhabitants and their islands became, increasingly, distinctly Hawaiian.

We know from our genealogical cosmologies that we as
Hawaiians descend directly from Papahānaumokuākea (a female
deity, literally "the substrate that gives birth to the expansive
islands"), Wākea (a male deity who is the expanse of the sky),
Hoʻohōkūkalani (the female deity who populates the night sky),
and Hāloanakalaukapalili (Hāloa of the quivering leaf), who is
the first *kalo* (taro) plant and elder brother of the first Hawaiian
man, from whom we all descend. This cosmology amplifies the
concept that it is through our generational interactions with
the biophysical elements of this place that our ancestors became
kānaka maoli, the people of this land, or Hawaiians.

For those of us who grew up with the traditions of our
island places and who have gone on to study, document, and
perpetuate our ancestors' practices, the divergent evolution of
lands and cultures across the archipelago is apparent. In this
chapter, we attempt to illuminate some of these important
place-specific adaptations of our people's social-environmental
systems in an attempt to bring a nuanced understanding of
Hawaiian resource management. The concept of our inherent
kinship with place is beginning to permeate the conservation
field in Hawai'i, elevating not only the knowledge of our biophysical world but the deep generational beliefs framed as
natural edicts and guidelines that once governed how our whole
society would interact with *ʻāina*, the inhabited land.

Over the past 20 years there has been a significant shift in
the social climate of Hawai'i, particularly within the conservation community. While just a generation ago, Hawaiian culture
was scarcely mentioned within the resource management sector,

today it is embedded into virtually every conservation plan. However, particularly within the institutions tasked with stewarding Hawai'i's land, the incorporation of cultural perspectives in resource management tends to rely on blanket concepts. For instance, the *ahupua'a*-based approach to land management has become synonymous with Hawaiian resource management practices as a whole, but the concept of an *ahupua'a*, imagined as in the poster, is highly simplified. A classic watershed situated within a valley and centered on a river is rarely found. In reality, *ahupua'a* may be bounded by streams, or run oblique to intermittent surface streams, or occur in areas without any streams at all, yet they remain an important feature of Hawaiian resource management despite their variations. Consequently, bringing attention to the diversity of place-based adaptations in Hawaiian society is timely. Recently there has been increased thinking in connection with other scales of Hawaiian resource management, particularly the larger *moku* land divisions, including applications that would restore management at this scale to address conservation issues today.

Currently, at the grassroots level many Hawaiian communities are implementing new methods and practices of conservation tailored to specific needs of *'āina*, of inhabited land, but conceiving of it broadly in terms of the word's literal translation, "that which feeds"—in effect, including land, sea, and society. These communities are pushing for new social-environmental systems adapted to the present and capable of adapting for the future. Central to these efforts is learning and reinvigorating the practices and identity of each distinct place as our ancestors did.

Here we present an overview of two contrasting areas of Hawai'i, situated at the opposite ends of the archipelago, to showcase similarities and differences in their social-environmental systems, highlighting cases where foundational concepts in

Hawaiian resource management, when utilized across vastly different landscapes, resulted in the emergence of divergent practices. We close by thinking explicitly about how these aspects of our past can and should influence contemporary resource management.

Ka Hana (Work): Approach

To understand the local social-environmental systems, we, like our mentors, draw on a diversity of approaches in our research, but include new methods and approaches not available to generations before us. First and foremost, each of us is guided by our elders and ancestors and ongoing relationships with *'āina*. We each are practitioners of *'āina*-based practices, from farming and feeding, to weaving, chanting, and engaging in ritual and hula, to crafting and giving leis. These practices motivate and intersect with our academic research, and we all return frequently to nurture and work the *'āina* that continues to nourish, inspire, and guide our work.

This discussion is based on case studies made where we come from or reside, conducted over the course of multiple decades, and enhanced and informed by the work of many other scholars. Our case studies are carried out with mixed methods, including analyses of Hawaiian-language newspaper articles, readings of secondary source texts on Hawaiian eco-systems and their uses, and employment of other historic research. In addition, we collect and analyze samples of soil, water, and seaweed, make extensive use of field trials, learn from contemporary restoration efforts by Hawaiian community groups, manage and steward varying ecosystems and cultural landscapes, and engage in interviews, surveys, focus groups, and participatory mapping with elders, practitioners, youth, fishers, and farmers. We draw upon the fields of archaeology, paleoecology, and biogeochemistry through published works as well as through investigations of our own. Often we use spatially explicit modeling to help bring parts of our research together to understand larger patterns of practices and application across a region or archipelago.

Ka Wahi (Sites): Where We Work

There are many storied areas of Hawai'i that could exemplify the intertwining of people and place that transforms *honua*, land, into *'āina*, that which feeds. While both *honua* and *'āina* can be translated to mean land, it is *'āina* that recognizes the integral connection between land and people. David Malo, an influential Hawaiian scholar writing between 1841 and 1853, wrote that land did not become *'āina* unless people were living there (*"ma ka noho ana, a kanaka, ua kapa ia, he aina ka inoa"*). *'Āina* recognizes that we are *kama'āina*, children of the land, shaped by our place as we are by every ancestor that came before us; it acknowledges that through our actions we not only shape the land but thereby shape ourselves.

To illustrate these differences, we explore two regions in depth—the *moku* of Kona, located in the west of the island of Hawai'i, and the *moku* of Halele'a and Ko'olau, located along the north shore of the island of Kaua'i. In terms of ecology, these sites are opposite in many ways. Kona is extremely young, having grown from lava flows less than 20,000 years old, and is located on the moderately dry, frequently lava-covered slopes of two volcanoes, Mauna Loa and Hualalai (figure 3.2). The volcanic eruptions that built Kaua'i occurred about 4.5 million years ago, and both of the Kaua'i *moku* are wet, receiving from 1,500 to 9,000 millimeters of rainfall per year, and have deep valleys carved by surface streams (see figure 3.3). Kona has no perennial surface streams; rather, it has subterranean water and

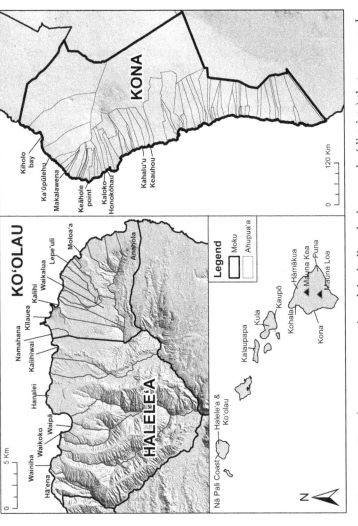

Figure 3.2. Key place-names mentioned, including the large *moku* (districts) that composed the study areas, several of the *ahupua'a* within those *moku*, and other referenced geographic and social features.

springs. Halele'a and Ko'olau have fringing reefs along much of the coast, which is also cut by large sandy bays, while Kona has a rocky coastline and deep ocean dropoffs near the shore. The trade winds that are prevalent in the Kaua'i *moku* are occluded in Kona.

Aspects of social resource management tailored to these contrasting environments illustrates how our ancestors applied common values and strategies relating to resources yet developed new strategies and practices in relation to different landscapes. Where applicable, we highlight specific examples from other locations across the archipelago to demonstrate the breadth of cultural evolution seen in the Hawaiian Islands.

Ka 'Ohi (Gathering): Comparative Case Study
KA HIKINA (ARRIVAL): LAND AND SEASCAPES

Our ancestors, the first *kānaka* to set foot upon the land that would come to be called Kona, found a place unlike any other part of the archipelago. Situated on the largest and southernmost island in the archipelago, the expansive Kona landscape embodies the vastness of both land and ocean. The *kānaka* discovered a patchwork of young lava flows sheltered by three large mountains, one of which is the tallest in the Pacific. Our ancestors observed that these mountains blocked the trade winds that blow onto the other side of the island and that this place, Kona, has its own weather system driven by the sun. The overhead summer sun heats the land and draws air in from the ocean, which cools, producing rain, as it rises up the slopes. Because of this localized weather pattern, Kona is the only area in the Hawaiian Islands that has more rainfall in the summer than in the winter.

Our ancestors went toward the mountains and found slopes covered with rocks, moss, trees and other plants, birds, and water. They saw that the young landscape had no perennial streams and that the wet uplands fed a strong groundwater system that resulted in many springs in the lowland and coastal/nearshore areas. They found that caves, some of the first sites of habitation, offered cool protection from the landscape of heated stone. Such caves are the many lava tubes scattered across the slopes. Later they found that the best building material for shelters was blocks of lava rock broken from the young *pāhoehoe* (smooth and ropy-textured) lava.

At the coast, our ancestors found rocky terrain with minimal nearshore reef development; the sea floor dropped off precipitously, giving rapid access to deepwater and pelagic fishing just offshore. They noticed that although amounts of soil varied across the landscape, the young lava rock substrate was highly fertile. They determined that the fresh water that moved underground was also fertile, enriched by nutrients as the young substrate through which it passed broke down, creating a productive coastline with an abundance and variety of algae, intertidal invertebrates, and nearshore animals. Important large pelagic species like yellowfin tuna, skipjack tuna, and marlin were right offshore.

At the other end of the Hawaiian archipelago, families thrived on the old, wet, and storied *moku* of Halele'a and Ko'olau on the geologically ancient island of Kaua'i. Its people refer affectionately to the island as Kaua'i Kuapapa (Kaua'i the oldest), acknowledging it as a foundational space on the archipelago. Beyond Kaua'i to the northwest is a series of much smaller islands that now anchor the world's largest marine national monument, starting with Nīhoa and Mokumanamana (Necker) and going all the way past Pihemanu (Midway). Kaua'i is considered the largest of this lineage of islands, and the families of Halele'a regularly returned to these small and distant islands on their oceangoing canoes, although the islands were never permanently inhabited.

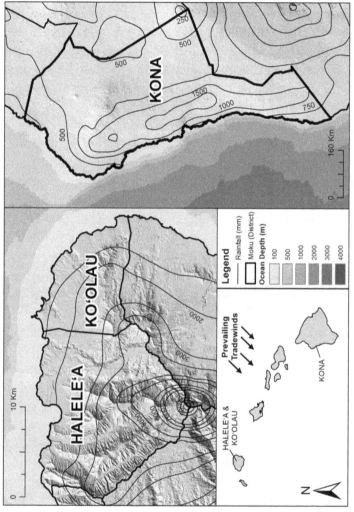

Figure 3.3. Key environmental features of the landscapes discussed here, including topography, rainfall, prevailing trade winds, and bathymetry.

The people called one of their *moku* Ko'olau for the predominant northeasterly trade winds (also named *ko'olau*) that this land directly faces (figure 3.3). These trade winds bring an abundance of rain throughout the year. They named the adjacent *moku* Halele'a, meaning "joyful house," a name thought to be linked to the area's profusion of water. Halele'a begins at Kalihiwai, meaning "edge of fresh water," and continues across nine *ahupua'a*, each watered by a sizable river or perennial stream. The people of these valley lands experienced huge amounts of rainfall. They referred to the highest mountain on Kaua'i, located at the back of the Hanalei and Wainiha valleys, as Wai'ale'ale, "rippling water." It is one of the wettest spots in Hawai'i and in the world.

Kānaka homes and agricultural patches dotted the coastline at the mouths of the rivers and streams. The coastline includes some of the most extensive reef systems in the Hawaiian Islands. It was here in the nearshore fisheries that important components of this community's diet were obtained. The water from the land also fed the ocean, resulting in a rich diversity of seaweed, which provided the people with valuable nutrients, such as iron. *Kānaka* methodically harvested many species of seaweed, understanding each species in great detail and appreciating that the taste of the seaweed changed from one patch of reef to another. It was primarily women who harvested seaweed and gathered reef species such as octopus, sea urchin, and crab, with reef fish such as Hawaiian chub and convict tang also composing a vital daily food source. It was said that "*maika'i Kaua'i hemolele i ka mālie*" (Kaua'i is beautiful, perfect in the calm). It was indeed a peaceful and an abundant place.

KA ʻĀINA (LAND THAT FEEDS): TRANSFORMATION
THROUGH HABITATION

Over time, *kānaka* engineered the landscape to manage its productive capacity, ultimately turning it into *ʻāina*, inhabited and
altered land that feeds. In Kona, where the easily accessible slopes
had gradients of rainfall, the *makaʻāinana* (people of the land)
utilized each portion of the landscape to their advantage while
maintaining strict rules that protected the resources from overexploitation. The rocky leeward coastline of Kona gives way
rapidly to deep waters, a situation that the fishers celebrated as
Kona o ke kai malino, Kona of the calm ocean. Stone-walled fishponds that were developed as a local innovation within Hawaiʻi
were difficult to construct in the deep water except in a few select
locations (famous ponds include Kīholo, Keāhole, Makalawena,
Kaloko, and Honokōhau). However, the lava tubes that carry
underground rivers from the uplands powered abundant springs
and freshwater ponds and pools. Productive aquaculture was
incorporated by protecting and augmenting nearshore and inland
pools and lakes, which, like the famous royal fishpond at Kīholo,
could be large. The relative lack of reefs and relative ease of access
to deepwater-supported fishing methods capitalized on pelagic
and other mid-depth species. After observing the natural patterns
(weather, freshwater flow, currents, activity on lower trophic
levels) that created the aggregation areas of large fish schools, a
dense network of underwater fishing spots was developed where
the fish would be fed and trained so that they could be called to
the nets when the time to harvest came. Hereditary chiefs insti-
tuted rules of resource interaction, including ascribing and enforc-
ing *kapu* (sacredness) and *kānāwai* (laws, rules, or protocols to
implement *kapu*) to ensure the perpetuation of these resources.
In the case of the ocean, there were rules that forbade the
seasonal take of species like big-eye scad and mackerel scad. While

the schools would be managed year-round, the harvest would occur only during a short period, during which stores would be dried in the hot Kona sun.

Because resources changed seasonally in Kona, the people moved seasonally, spending some of the year in the uplands and some of the year near the sea. The dry parts of Kona were famous for salt production, with people taking advantage of the sun in late winter after heavy surf cleaned and filled pools along the rocky coastline. The people carved out and smoothed rock into depressions to serve as catchments, using rocks and a mortar made from heating crushed coral.

The farmers of Kona developed myriad agricultural forms, using, almost exclusively, plants brought by the discoverers on canoes. From the coast to the uplands farmers established zones of agriculture that took advantage of the changing ecology of the land (figure 3.4). Along the drier coast, there were dense settlements with well-tended gardens and trees watered by groundwater. However, most of the productive land was situated well inland from the coast.

The dry coastal plains were utilized for drought-tolerant resource plants, mainly *pili* grass (*Heteropogon contortus*, thatching grass), along with *noni* (*Morinda citrifolia*, Indian mulberry), *hala* (*Pandanus tectorius*, screwpine), *niu* (*Cocos nucifera*, the coconut palm), and *ipu* (*Lagenaria siceraria*, the bottle gourd). Further upland, *kānaka* took advantage of the increased, but highly variable from year to year, rainfall to create a forest zone dominated by breadfruit; it was known as the breadfruit grove. The hardy breadfruit trees, associated with prosperity, often were cultivated on young lava flows with shallow soils; there, the trees provided habitat and mulch for crops cultivated in their shade, such as the high-quality paper mulberry, whose bark was pounded into *kapa* cloth for clothes and other linen.

Figure 3.4. An artist's illustration of the social-ecological landscape of Kona, a region without river valleys, prior to foreign influences. Bishop Museum Archives. Reproduced with permission from the Bishop Museum (www.bishopmuseum.org).

Upslope of the breadfruit groves, rainfall was still greater; here *kānaka* worked tirelessly, often in the morning or even at night to avoid the Kona heat, to create an extensive network of stonework that framed the prized gardens of the most intensively cultivated food plants. The farmers used diversified agricultural systems to manage sun, water, and nutrients for the production of staple crops and resources such as *kalo* (taro), *'uala* (*Ipomoea batatas*, sweet potato), *'uhi* (*Dioscorea alata*, the greater yam), *mai'a* (*Musa spp.*, banana/plantain), and *kī* (*Cordyline terminalis,* or ti). Although practices were shared and perpetuated through stories, each plot was adapted to the conditions created by the patchwork of lava flows and micro habitats.

As the rainfall increased farther upslope, the fertility of the soils declined and the distance to the coast increased until the farmers no longer invested in a large-scale conversion of the landscape. At the lower margin of the native forest, *kānaka* made use of nutrients cycled by the forest by leaving the forest canopy intact and planting food and other resource crops in the understory, as well as encouraging and harvesting desired resource plants already growing there.

At still higher elevations on the forested slopes of Hualālai and Mauna Loa, the managed and tended landscape gave way to unaltered forest, which was considered the realm of the gods. An average *kānaka* would rarely, if ever, enter the forest and then only for very special functions, such as to harvest specific resources that were protected and governed by strict rules. Organized by local experts, occasional expeditions might seek out exceptionally large *koa* (*Acacia koa*) trees, which were prized for making canoes. Trained specialists in the employment of the hereditary chiefs would also make seasonal trips to harvest the highly prized feathers of honeycreepers (an endemic— found only in Hawai'i—family of birds), used in the creation of royal insignia.

In Halele'a and Ko'olau on Kaua'i, the abundance of water fostered the development of large systems of *lo'i kalo* (taro paddies) that covered much of the floor of the larger valleys. Centers of irrigated *lo'i kalo* cultivation included Hanalei, still known today as Hawai'i's largest *kalo*-producing area, along with other substantial valleys. Dryer areas of Ko'olau, with intermittent streams or where water came mainly from springs, also had smaller areas of *loʻi kalo* as well as rain-fed cultivation of *ʻuala* (sweet potato), which was cultivated in areas such as the Kīlauea and Anahola plains. In these *moku* it was not uncommon to develop paddies in sandy soils directly adjacent to the ocean.

There are records of family cultivation of areas in the reef, just as there are records of families cultivating upland agricultural plots. Families gathered marine resources from small stretches of reef, giving these spots names to characterize, delineate, and solidify familial relationships with them. Well into the 1980s and even the 1990s, people were expected to respect these familial gathering areas and stick to their own family areas. Elders raised in the 1920s, 1930s, and 1940s were strong in their agreement that they never fished outside their own *ahupuaʻa* and left areas claimed by other families within their own *ahupuaʻa* alone, for there was more than enough diversity and plenty of seafood on their own reef patches. It was considered a sign of poor caretaking and disrespect to venture into others' reef areas, akin to how we today would regard venturing into another family's refrigerator without asking. In interviews, elders referred to such caretaking practices as protecting particular stages in a fish's lifecycle—not harvesting the largest individuals of a given species (those that reproduce the most), protecting certain areas as hatcheries for baby fish, and not harvesting fish with eggs. In one community of Haleleʻa, community members have worked with the government to create state law based on some of these Indigenous conservation-based fishing practices through creation of a community-based subsistence fishing area, or CBSFA, the first in the state of Hawaiʻi, established in 2016.

Elders remember having to tend beds of *limu kohu* (*Asparagopsis taxiformis*, a red alga that was particularly favored for eating) in the spring, prior to its reproductive period, removing weedy and invasive species, or "rubbish seaweed," and old growth to create space for new spores to settle. Families also made use of *imu kai,* a technique documented particularly for Hā'ena in which stones are aggregated and piled just offshore. Fish seek shelter in the structure and can be harvested easily by surrounding the stone pile with a small net and removing the stones. This technique, along with fishpond aquaculture, provides a steady source of protein even in the winter, when ocean swells are high in coastal areas and fishing on outer reefs becomes dangerous.

Fishponds for aquaculture took different forms in Halele'a and Ko'olau than in other areas. These include ponds separated from the ocean by a berm of sand, a form used in sandier Halele'a. Inland there were freshwater fishponds. Along the rockier shores of Ko'olau, *kānaka* also made fish traps that were rough rock enclosures that marine fish could enter—an older practice that, unlike the creation of reef-flat fishponds, is also found elsewhere in the Pacific.

KA PĀLENA (BOUNDARIES): LAND DIVISIONS AND THEIR IMPLICATIONS

Long before European contact, Hawaiian society divided lands in a hierarchical pattern. The following scales of division are consistently recognized and retain some meaning into the present— *mokupuni, moku, ahupua'a,* and '*ili. Mokupuni,* the largest, at the island scale, were at times managed by a paramount chief; they comprise multiple *moku. Moku,* large land divisions like Kona, Ko'olau, and Halele'a, contain multiple *ahupua'a. Moku* were ruled by lesser chiefs, who were either independent or chosen by the paramount chief. Most *kānaka* lived within and gathered resources from *ahupua'a.* The *ahupua'a* managers interceded between the chiefs who appointed them and the people—just as chiefs interceded between *kānaka* and *akua* (elemental deities). The *'ili* were typically lands managed and used at the family level.

This system of land division, often described in shorthand as the *ahupua'a* system, functioned for resource management, resource distribution, and the organization and control of society. The development of the *ahupua'a* system is associated with the famous O'ahu chief Ma'ilikūkahi, but the system appears to have spread rapidly to all of the islands in the archipelago. It was the basis for the nation of Hawai'i, in which relatively autonomous local-level resource governance was balanced by district- and island-level authorities. The creation of a Hawaiian monarchy at the archipelago scale did not occur until more than a quarter-century after European contact and relied on allegiances with and weapons from foreigners. The monarchy, formally recognized by other nineteenth-century world governments, added an additional hierarchical level to this already functioning sociopolitical system.

In Kona, the initial establishment of *ahupua'a* is often associated with 'Umialīloa, the famous farmer-chief who established Kona as the royal center of the island. During the reign of 'Umialīloa the island was unified and great public works were organized and established. The Kona *ahupua'a*, and Hawai'i Island *ahupua'a* in general, tend to not extend to mountain peaks. Typically, only one or a handful of *ahupua'a* within each region extend to the uplands, where they expand to encompass the entire peak area of the region. Many other *ahupua'a* tend to live under the "umbrella" of these key *ahupua'a*, their upper boundary being truncated within or just above the upland forest region; for an example of this umbrella layout, see the Keauhou *ahupua'a* in the Kona *moku* in figure 3.2. This layout suggests a level of control of the lesser *ahupua'a* by the larger ones that cap them. This pattern can also be seen at a smaller scale, where individual *ahupuaʻa* are carved out of larger ones, with the smaller, younger *ahupuaʻa* overarched by their big brothers. Extensions and reshapings of *ahupuaʻa* result in a huge variation in *ahupuaʻa* size, from a mere 134 hectares for Kaʻoheʻiki to more than 25,000 hectares for Puʻuanahulu.

A system known as *lele* (jumping or flying) was common in Kona. A single family could have responsibility for and rights to multiple unconnected parcels that "jumped" across the landscape, which allowed the family to have access to the ocean, the lowlands, and the prime agricultural uplands. At the time of the *Māhele,* the initial privatization of land, beginning in 1848 in the Kingdom of Hawaiʻi, most families were awarded three to five land parcels, which was indicative of the *lele* system. Even within Kona, families would have different relationships and interactions with their parcels as the landscape varied. In the south, which has somewhat steeper slopes and higher rainfall bands closer to the coast, a family could live by the coast and, within an hour or two, hike to the uppermost reaches of the managed landscape. Many elders still recount having to hike along the trails with their grandparents to tend their *kalo* patches in the uplands. In the north, where the volcano Hualālai creates long slopes and the high-rainfall zone retreats farther uphill, access to family lands became more seasonal than daily. For instance, in the *ahupuaʻa* of Kaʻūpūlehu, the shoreline was occupied in the late winter and spring when fish and seaweed were abundant and the summer rains had not yet anointed the uplands for planting. When the rains began in the summer, labor was needed in the far upland agricultural lands, and people moved there.

The huge size of Hawaiʻi Island compared to the other islands suggests that it was harder for one paramount chief to control the entire territory. Indeed, through much of Hawaiʻi's history the island was ruled at the *moku* level rather than as a single unit, and two to four paramount chiefs shared control of the island. As power was consolidated and individuals gained control of regions, the paramount chiefs granted power and land to them, and these lesser chiefs did the same in turn, which created a hierarchical management system that increased the number of chief families with places within the structure, thereby reducing the potential for conflict.

On Kauaʻi, development of the *moku* and *ahupuaʻa* system is attributed to the great ruler Manōkalanipō, whose reign heralded a time of peace and abundance. Although paramount chiefs of Kauaʻi tended to base their courts at the sacred Wailua *moku* on the eastern side of the island, local chiefs of *moku* and even of *ahupuaʻa* maintained great autonomy in their regions, and names of local leaders, such as Lohiʻau of Hāʻena, are remembered in stories and legends.

Unlike in Kona, most of the *ahupuaʻa* of Haleleʻa and Koʻolau stretch from mountain peak to the sea. However, many contain multiple watersheds within their boundaries, and some have side boundaries that follow, not ridges, but the paths of rivers, which creates a diversity of *ahupuaʻa* even in an area of more classically shaped topography (river valleys with steep valley ridges). Some smaller areas within valleys occur as *ahupuaʻa,* which appear to have been carved out later in history from other valleys and reach only to ridges, not peaks. These smaller *ahupuaʻa* may have resulted from the political redistribution of lands that occurred after the island was ceded peacefully to Kamehameha, the paramount chief of Hawaiʻi Island, early in the nineteenth century. Examples include Namahana and Waikoko, both of which were given in their entirety as royal patent grants during the *Māhele.*

Ahupuaʻa in Koʻolau and Haleleʻa range in size from Wainiha Valley, with over 6,000 hectares, to Waipā, with 160 hectares. Land awards issued for *moku* generally show two parcels per tenant, one a house lot, often located toward the sea, and the other a *lo'i* (paddy or pondfield), located farther back on the alluvial plain within the valley, accessed by trail or boat. Beyond a family's *kuleana* land—land to and for which an individual family had rights and responsibilities—a family was able to access lands of its *ahupua'a* for timber, medicine, thatch, and other products, as well as the *ahupua'a*'s nearshore fisheries. Most families both farmed and fished, providing for their daily needs more or less self-sufficiently. The distance from upland resources to the seaside could be traversed easily within a day, or even multiple times a day, and in some elder accounts, farmers could harvest *kalo* from their paddies early in the morning, set the tubers on a fire to steam, head to the ocean to catch fish, and return in time to eat fish and *kalo* for lunch. In Ko'olau and Halele'a, upland-to-seaside trade for staples was less prevalent perhaps than in other regions with larger *ahupua'a*, such as within the *moku* of Kula on Maui Island, where upland farming was separated from the coast by nearly 18 kilometers; there, families often lived in either the uplands or the coastal areas, which necessitated trading to access the full suite of resources within the *ahupua'a*.

KA 'EA (GOVERNANCE): SOCIOPOLITICAL ADAPTATION

Kona's heavy reliance on rain-fed agriculture and arboriculture, as opposed to the reliance of most regions of Hawai'i on irrigated agriculture and managed aquaculture, contributed to the emergence of unique practices, some of which spread across the islands. For instance, the development of the *kō'ele* system of taxation is associated with the Kona region. A more conventional taxation system involved the hereditary chiefs claiming, at their discretion, part of the production from local farmers and fishers through specific ceremonies. The *kō'ele* system, in contrast, was a tax paid in labor. The chief's lands were set aside and worked and maintained by the local community under the direction of an *ahupua'a* overseer, with the production of those lands being reserved for the chief. This system created a fair balance between taxation and production, because in a bad year the chief's lands would be affected the same as those of the farmers. Also, the *kō'ele* system allowed the mobilization of labor to build infrastructure.

The emergence of the Makahiki festival, which grew to be the paramount religious ceremony across the archipelago, also occurred in the Kona region. Here, a multiweek ceremonial period was observed, with its timing marked by the position of the Pleiades. Two key practices embody the essence of this festival as relates to governance. First, the festival period was war-free. Harvest and planting could be conducted without fear, helping to ensure the quality and quantity of food for everyone. Second, an island-wide royal procession was held in which visits to and assessments from all the individual *ahupua'a* were conducted. This procession was marked by challenges and games that assessed the vigor of the population, as well as gifts and homage from the common people to the chiefs that reflected local productivity that year.

Being so heavily reliant on rainfall, the Kona region had substantial year-to-year variation in food production and (we believe not coincidentally) fostered an exceptional development of political aspirations, evinced in both warfare and political alliances. The turnover of the families of hereditary chiefs over time, as well as the relative number of intermarriages between chiefs' families, was much greater on Hawai'i Island than it was on other islands in the archipelago. Both of these observations suggest that vying for power was likely more intense on Hawai'i Island than elsewhere, as was the need to retain power during times of peace. Kamehameha I, who launched the most successful military campaign in the history of the islands and established an archipelago-wide monarchy following European contact, governed from Kona as the seat of his royal court.

Trade across *ahupua'a* and even across islands provided access to goods whose source was specific *ahupua'a* or islands, such as certain fish species, prized sea salt from Hanapēpē on Kaua'i Island, stone quarried from above the treeline on Mauna Kea (where it had been pushed out under glacial ice) to use for creating adzes, and large *koa* trunks from Hawai'i Island for building canoes. On Hawai'i Island, the summer crop-growing season of Kona likely supported seasonal sharing between neighboring *moku*, as well as trade within the *moku* of salt and upland crops. Similar exchange has continued in more recent times; oral histories document the trade of fish from Halele'a for salt from Hanapēpē and the sharing of fish from the *ahupua'a* of Hā'ena with family and friends across the island—and even with Hawaiian families from the area who had moved to the North American continent. Those species that are harder to find in other parts of Kaua'i, such as *'o'io* (bonefish, *Albula vulpes*), are shared more widely than are commonly dispersed species such as *akule* (mackerel scad, *Decapterus macarellus*). While the roadless Nāpali coast on the western margin of Halele'a is seen in contemporary times as a barrier to travel around Kaua'i, the valleys of Nāpali were home to thriving communities connected to outside communities to the west and north by canoe, as well as by extensive trail systems that included ladders to scale vertical cliffs. There is considerable archaeological evidence for a gathering place on the Nāpali coast for games and ceremonies during the Makahiki festival season. Many families of both Waimea and Hā'ena moved from Nāpali *ahupua'a* after the population collapse that followed European contact, when towns like Waimea and Hanalei became thriving ports that offered modern medicine, economic opportunities, and schools founded by missionaries.

Ahupua'a overseers, or *konohiki,* played an important role on Kaua'i as lesser chiefs overseeing harvests and irrigation systems in individual *ahupua'a.* Some overseers were women, like Lohi'au's sister, Kahua, in the *ahupua'a* of Hā'ena, referenced in the famous story of Hi'iakaikapoliopele. In the *moku* of Ko'olau there is at least one early newspaper article referencing multiple overseers for one *ahupua'a* at the same time. The article suggests that different overseers were selected by different means and played different roles. One was appointed by the paramount chief of Kaua'i as his representative and was referred to as a tax collector. The overseer of the people appeared to be a respected community member, selected for his or her knowledge and character, who supervised collective fishing and work projects, mediated disputes, and undertook similar tasks. It is unclear whether this diversity of roles in governance endured across centuries and *ahupua'a* throughout these two districts or whether it occurred only at a specific place and time. Very few individuals could be expected to combine expertise in managing fisheries with ability to resolve disputes, allocate water, understand soil fertility, and deal with all the other aspects of community life.

Kaua'i generally, and the *moku* of Ko'olau and Halele'a in particular, is striking in its abundance of food and in the relative ease with which a surplus of food could be produced over and above the subsistence needs of those farming and fishing. That abundance, and that surplus, made it possible to support societies in which many individuals could play roles other than farmer or fisher. Their societies could include teachers, dancers, artists, and warriors. The existence of a surplus would have made the conquest of Kaua'i appealing, especially to hereditary chiefs from the highly variable lands of Kona. At the same time, the ability to use that surplus to maintain a body of well-trained warriors would have made conquest difficult. At least twice in the history of the archipelago, chiefs from Hawai'i Island succeeded in conquering every other island but Kaua'i.

Ka 'Ike (Knowledge, That Which Is Seen): Discussion

Looking back at the classic *ahupua'a* concept embodied in the "Ahupua'a Poster" (see figure 3.1), we see that its comprehensibility is attractive, as is its alignment with Western watershed management systems. The poster portrays units of Hawaiian interaction with pie-shaped sections of land centered on a river or stream and bounded by mountain ridges; the water is diverted through a series of paddies for agriculture and empties into a shallow nearshore environment with walled-in fishponds for aquaculture. The native forest in the uplands gives way to managed forests in the mid-elevations, with houses and other constructed features occurring exclusively at the coasts. Yet as we have seen, generic concepts, including that of the classic *ahupua'a*, do not apply universally across the archipelago. Still, some underlying conceptual themes are foundational across the *moku* we study. We close by describing these themes, but not so that they may be used to define and bound *kānaka* relationships with their land. Instead, they may serve to bind together many distinct relationships, experiences, and practices of our people to place and so provide a lens through which to see and understand them more clearly as we islanders continue to reinvigorate and adapt.

KA WAI (WATER), KA WAIWAI (WEALTH)

Although watersheds are often not the defining unit of land division in Hawai'i, fresh water is central in shaping social-environmental systems and management practices. As shown in Kona, the identification of *ahupua'a* as watersheds does not apply to geologically younger landscapes where rivers and ridges do not exist. However, even in areas where soils were developed sufficiently and the land was eroded sufficiently to have surface water, *ahupua'a* did not always align with watersheds. As we saw, both Ko'olau and Halele'a on Kaua'i have *ahupua'a* that encompass several watersheds or a smaller area of land within a single watershed. Elsewhere, for example in the high-rainfall Hāmākua region along the northeast coast of Hawai'i Island, surface streams typically serve as *ahupua'a* boundaries, rather than running through their center, and some streams even traverse multiple *ahupua'a*. In the leeward Kohala region along the northwest coast of Hawai'i Island, flowing surface water does not appear to have been a defining resource, for the intermittent waterways cut diagonally across *ahupua'a*.

We suggest that our ancestors situated *ahupua'a* as a function, not of watersheds exclusively, but of fresh water in all its forms, including clouds, mist, groundwater, springs, dew, and rain. The paramount importance of fresh water (*wai*) in Hawaiian epistemology is evident in the reduplication of the word to become *waiwai*, which can mean "goods, property, assets, valuables, value, worth, wealth, importance, benefit, estate, use." That the root word of "value," "worth," and "wealth" is "water" signifies its vitality in the Hawaiian mind and in *kānaka* systems of land use. We suggest that the delineation of *ahupua'a* locations and boundaries was based on an understanding of varied regional sources of water and the complex processes through which these sources nourished certain *'āina*.

In the south Kona region, for instance, the *ahupua'a* of Keauhou extends into the uplands and includes a swath of land in the saddle between the summits of Hualālai and Mauna Loa, creating an umbrella over the *ahupua'a* to the north and south (see figure 3.2). Such an umbrella is a common occurrence on

Hawai'i Island, indicating a level of political control. Indeed, Keauhou was the primary seat of royal power in Kona. However, Keauhou does not extend throughout the entire *moku* of Kona; Kona *ahupuaʻa* to both the far north and the south fall outside its umbrella. The extent of Keauhou, however, aligns well with the cloud bank created by the local convection-driven weather pattern captured by Mauna Loa and Hualālai. This division of land appears to be driven by knowledge of fresh water in the form of clouds and rain, a knowledge most appropriate in a region reliant on rain-fed agriculture. The boundaries of Keauhou and the cloud bank also align with land use. For instance, the extent of the breadfruit grove aligns perfectly with the cloud bank and consequently with the upland extension of Keauhou.

The *ahupuaʻa* in the more northern parts of Kona, where the landscape becomes considerably drier, are centered predominantly around significant bays. Although the ocean itself, being salty, is not a source of fresh water, the bays typically have groundwater discharge. Significant springs in each bay provide for the needs of *kānaka* while enriching the ocean with nutrients from the land and enhancing availability of food. Indeed, this flow of subterranean fresh water powers the processes that cause the bays to form, centering *ahupuaʻa* divisions on yet another form of fresh water—subterranean flow, groundwater tables, and springs.

Some regions are less clear in how they relate to fresh water. The leeward *ahupuaʻa* of the Kohala region on the northwest part of Hawai'i Island may show adaptation of land management divisions to fresh water as mist. Here, the intermittent waterways run diagonally through the *ahupuaʻa*. Both scientific studies and Indigenous knowledge highlight the importance of windborne mist as a major, if not the dominant, source of moisture for agriculture in this region. Linear mounds in the agricultural fields, running perpendicular to the prevailing winds, were planted with flexible stalks of *kō* (*Saccharum officinarum*, sugarcane). The stalks acted as mist traps, capturing and concentrating moisture that otherwise would have blown across the landscape and out to sea. The *ahupuaʻa* boundaries run largely parallel to the trade winds, possibly in recognition of this very particular form of fresh water. These examples show the intricacies and variation of *kānaka* systems adapted to manage water as a foundational resource.

KA MAHIʻAI (CULTIVATOR, TO CULTIVATE)

Just as forms of water and traditional water management varied, agricultural systems across the archipelago reflected adaptations to many types of ecosystem. Hawaiian agricultural strategies were highly diverse, including *loʻi* (paddies for *kalo*), rain-fed cropping (mainly for *kalo* and *ʻuala*), arboriculture/ agroforestry), swidden agriculture, and more. The forms of agriculture differed in their products, yields, and resilience.

Within farmed areas, adaptation to the landscape can be seen at macro, meso, and micro levels. At the macro level, each form of agriculture was developed in partnership with what the land offered. Use of *loʻi* (paddies and pondfields) was an efficient system in which high inputs of labor for construction of agricultural capital were rewarded with long-lasting, high, and reliable yields with relatively low maintenance. *Kānaka* developed such *loʻi* everywhere that water could be gravitationally fed via the construction of irrigation canals and terraces. In rain-fed field systems, rock-derived minerals dissolve in water and break down as soils weather and age over time, with greater rainfall liberating elements (nutrients) that are essential to plant growth and creating invisible limits to sustained production. Throughout the archipelago, farmers identified and utilized areas with naturally elevated soil fertility. For instance, on the island of Moloka'i, which mostly has old lava lying under nutrient-depleted soils, farmers established an intensive rain-fed agricultural system only in a small region on the island that had resulted from a late-stage volcanic eruption and that therefore had younger and more fertile soils. However, these thresholds that constrain large, intensive rain-fed agricultural systems do not limit development of all forms of agriculture. In Kona we see farming of the forest understory in wetter areas where soil fertility was diminished. Here, farmers made use of naturally enhanced nutrient cycles of forested ecosystems, cycles driven by the uplift and recycling of nutrients by large trees.

The agricultural infrastructure that characterizes these systems is often the same, yet adapted for specific purposes in each region. The long linear mounds that are the hallmark of intensive dryland agriculture in Hawai'i appear to play different roles in hydrological function within the different systems. In the Kohala region, where their orientation is perpendicular to the strong prevailing winds, the mounds functioned to capture mist and break the wind. In contrast, in the Kona region the mounds run parallel to the less intense wind, suggesting a different function, one we hypothesize is related to managing water, sunlight, and evaporation rather than wind or wind-driven mist, as in Kohala. Within regions, the application of different cropping practices, built infrastructure, and forms of water management demonstrates specialized adaptations to the local environment that optimize the use of each zone of the landscape to enhance productivity.

Experienced farmers used ingenuity and infrastructure to expand the ecological boundaries of each of their agricultural forms. While *lo'i* systems are generally characterized as relying on irrigation from streams or springs, *kānaka* developed diverse means through which *lo'i* accessed water. In some areas, flooded systems were powered by cuts into hillsides to access groundwater. There is at least one historical account of *kalo* being grown on floating rafts in deep water. Natural wetland areas were also modified to encourage the flow of water to create agroecological systems. In transforming wetlands into *lo'i*, *kānaka* also expanded habitat for other useful species and food sources. In fact, some species of native waterbirds do not occur in the fossil record until after the establishment of intensive *lo'i* systems, which highlights the biocultural benefits of Native Hawaiian agricultural design and execution.

Under other extreme climate conditions, farmers provide another example of expanding the arable footprint. In dry areas, farmers built large rock mounds and small catchments to conserve and concentrate moisture and implemented planting regimes that were highly responsive to rainfall patterns. In high-rainfall, lower-fertility regions such as Hāmākua and Puna, our ancestors planted forests that enhanced fertility and sped landscape-scale nutrient cycling, improving the habitat for understory cultivation of other crops. In the swidden cultivation system of Hāmākua with its managed fallow, *kānaka* cultivated *kukui* (*Aleurites moluccanus*, or candlenut), trees that are fast growing and produce prolific, rapidly decomposing leaf litter, in order to build up soil fertility, which in turn powered the cultivation of other crops by enhancing soil fertility and promoting a more rapid return to the food production phase of shifting cultivation.

Temporal variation in management was another essential element in agricultural strategies. The establishment of plantings coincided with seasonal weather events that brought sufficient moisture for agriculture, with subsequent management focused on reducing evaporation and conserving moisture. A favorite saying associated with *'uala* is "*Ua ka ua, i hea 'oe?*" (When the rains came, where were you?) The phrase is meant to accuse someone of laziness, of disappearing when there is work to be done, and indicates how the work of planting sweet potato had to be timed with the onset of rains.

Although common practices such as maximizing use of high-nutrient areas, enhancing soil fertility, and maintaining moisture underpinned farming across Hawai'i, regional agricultural systems were adapted to local ecological conditions, and they incorporated place-based political and religious practices. *Kānaka* honored the same major *akua* (gods) across the archipelago—Kāne, Kū, Lono, Kanaloa, Haumea, Hina, among them—many of whom are also revered by our Pacific cousins under similar names. Yet different communities elevated certain gods in regard and devotion, along with their associated natural phenomena. In areas where *lo'i kalo* were the dominant form of agriculture, the god Kāne, representing energy associated with heat and moving fresh water, was often celebrated together with his related deities, while in communities where rain-fed agriculture was prominent, the god Lono, representing energy associated with wind, sound, and far-reaching storms, was more central. When we honor gods like Kāne or Lono, we are not honoring only a deity but actual fresh water, the actual sun that moves that water from our atmosphere into our forest, the very real storms that bring faraway weather to our paddies. Place-based knowledge and farmers' practices were perpetuated intergenerationally through *mo'olelo* and *ka'ao*—oral histories that encapsulated the knowledge and practices of each area. The elevation of individual gods codified the most salient elements of each place and its ecosystems into the religious and therefore political fabric of society, with hereditary chiefs exalted as the bridge between the people and the gods.

Although the design of agricultural systems and their associated practices, deities, and rituals differed greatly across the varied ecosystems of the Hawaiian archipelago, each form

of cultivation represented adaptation to place-specific ecological conditions from climate to topography to nutrient
availability in soils. In turn, *kānaka* agricultural innovations
changed the very landscapes to which they were adapted by
shaping hydrology, nutrient cycles, and sometimes topography
and by enhancing soil fertility.

Ka Huliau: Resurgence of *Kānaka Maoli* Social-Environmental Systems

The emphasis here has been on traditional social-environmental
systems of Hawai'i, systems that persist and are adapted today,
although they have become harder to observe because of the
influx of colonial powers.

Captain James Cook's first encounter with the Hawaiian
Islands—the first step toward colonization—occurred at
Waimea, on Kaua'i; the second, at Kealakekua Bay in Kona, on
Hawai'i Island. Shortly after those encounters, both locations
became centers of interaction with European ships. Approximately forty years later, missionaries arrived from the eastern
United States and began to set up churches and mission settlements across the islands. Early Westerners arriving in the islands
founded economic ventures, such as coffee plantations, silk-
worm farms, and, later, cattle ranches and sugar and pineapple
plantations, causing enormous changes in land use. Extensive
water diversions were created to support the monoculture
production of these thirsty cash crops. Foreign plantation and
ranch operations on large tracts of land brought foreign labor-
ers to Hawai'i, leading to the development of large new settlements. They also altered the Native community's ability to
access natural resources; *kānaka* often required special permission and a relationship with plantations and ranches to access
and harvest their crops. While many area residents retained

access well into the 1970s, the subsequent demise of plantation agriculture led to the division and sale of large tracts of agricultural land to private owners. This land continues to be divided into smaller tracts, sold, and resold to ever wealthier individuals. Privatization of land coupled with newer landowners' desire for privacy and lack of understanding of the history and customary rights of *kānaka* increases pressure on Native Hawaiian families who still live on ancestral lands and are faced with rising taxes and surrounding development pressures.

Community efforts to hold land in common provide a key means to perpetuate access and stewardship of natural resources. Such initiatives build upon early innovations, such as the community land groups (*hui*) that were founded in both Hā'ena and Wainiha in Halele'a during the 1850s through 1870s to hold land in common and buy back land from hereditary chiefs after the *Māhele*, the initial privatization of land. The constitution of the Wainiha Hui guarantees all members access to and through all the lands of Wainiha and the right to graze 20 head of cattle provided they do no damage to neighbors' crops.

More contemporary efforts include the Waipā Foundation's lease of Waipā *ahupua'a* from Kamehameha Schools. Once slated by Kamehameha Schools for the development of a Japanese-owned resort, the Waipā community pleaded their case for more Indigenous management with meaningful returns to their community. After creating a community-based nonprofit, the Waipā Foundation today is a center of culturally grounded community-based economic development, with cultivation of *kalo* and other crops and the production of *poi* (a staple food produced from *kalo*) and such value-added products as *poi* cheesecake and handmade sausage. Waipā's education programs and annual community summer program serve over 2,000 learners per year. In Hā'ena, the Hui Maka'āinana o Makana, comprising descendants of families who received land

in Hā'ena during the *Māhele* and founders of the original Hā'ena
Hui, have restored and continue to care for *lo'i* within the state
park at Kē'ē. Although most Hā'ena families can no longer af-
ford to live in Hā'ena, with its high-priced coastal luxury homes,
the Hui gathers twice a month to work at the *lo'i*, to hold fishing camps for area youth, and to host visiting government of-
ficials and other partners in co-management. Families of
Halele'a and Ko'olau, along with their many *hoa 'āina* (literally,
"friends of the land") continue to work toward a vision of a
future with many *kīpuka*—literally, areas of forest spared by a
lava flow, which figuratively refers to islands of culture, resurgence, and growth—a future with land governed by area families in each and every *ahupua'a* along the coast. The goal is a
self-governed and sustainable future for Hawai'i.

    Both Kona and Halele'a regions have passed substantial
community-based marine protection milestones in the past few
years. In Halele'a, many years of effort in organizing and peti-
tioning the state government culminated in the first permanent
community-based subsistence fishing area in Hawai'i, where
the community has written the management rules that are now
enacted into law. In Kona, a community-based group in
Ka'ūpūlehu, led by the lineal descendants in the *ahupua'a*,
worked for over 17 years to change the state of Hawai'i's admin-
istrative rules to create a 10-year "Try Wait" rest area, closed to
all harvest. The purpose of the rest area is to allow the nearshore
ecosystem, including important reef-fish stocks, to replenish
while the community develops a culturally grounded, sustainable harvest plan for the area to ensure that their descendants
have a reciprocal relationship with this seascape in perpetuity.
In both places, as in many other Hawai'i communities pursuing
formal designations for local management, proposed rules are
based upon place-specific ancestral practices underpinned by
principles shared in diverse communities across the archipelago.

Some of these principles include protecting spawning areas and times, resting crops and rotating harvests, limiting take and type of gear used, and caring for the harvested areas.

These efforts seeking to decentralize resource management are driven by Hawaiian communities across the archipelago, organized in networks of *kalo* farmers, fishpond cultivators, fishers, environmental educators, supporting academics, and nonprofit groups. This growing movement is a response to the centralization of the authority to govern natural resources over the century-plus since the illegal overthrow of the Hawaiian Kingdom in 1893. Legal authority to create and enforce regulations and implement management is largely centered within the underfunded, understaffed, overtasked Hawai'i State Department of Land and Natural Resources. *Kānaka* communities have watched the decline of lands and waters under state management and the failure of one-size-fits-all regulations. Although local-level resource management systems once functioned in balance with broader governance at multiple scales, today there is a vital need to rebalance by redistributing management authority to community groups through collaborative management regimes.

In the late 1980s, there were just a handful of community organizations caring for land and water refuges in Hawai'i. Today there are hundreds, many of which formed in just the past decade. Many of the founders of some of these younger groups and movements grew up in, and trained with, more established entities. One example is the *ahupua'a* of He'eia on O'ahu, where efforts to restore a fishpond at Paepae o He'eia have helped to spawn restoration of other fishponds within the *moku* of Ko'olau, O'ahu, as well as to generate organizations caring for *'āina* within He'eia from the mountains to the sea. These community groups employ a variety of mechanisms to establish access and authority to care for lands and waters, ranging from formal leases to curatorship and stewardship agreements to rights of entry to illegal occupation to open access for all to work on public lands. This growing grassroots movement from end to end of the Hawaiian archipelago reaffirms and restores place-based, responsive, and adaptive management of resources attuned to the highly different ecologies, temporal patterns, and social pressures on the landscape.

The notion of the universal *ahupuaʻa* encapsulated in the "Ahupuaʻa Poster" has done much to highlight valuable aspects of Hawaiian resource management. Nevertheless, there is so much more to understand of the nuances and ingenuity of *kānaka* adaptations to the diverse climates and landscapes of Hawaiʻi. There is no single way to encapsulate Hawaiian management, for each local area had its own challenges and opportunities. Adjusting the application of practices and restrictions developed and created in each region was crucial to survival and remains important today if we are to thrive.

There are, however, common underpinnings to the place-specific adaptations, which are rooted in a perspective of kinship with the *ʻāina*. Ongoing adaptation to the ever-more-rapid environmental changes of the present must be guided, like the innovations of our ancestors, by broad principles. Honor your place, your plant people, your animal people, your water systems that give you life. Observe your natural surroundings in days, months, seasons, years. Integrate from the mountains to the sea. Understand the ancestral resources, study the ancestral laws that guide your interactions, and establish your boundaries with those resources. Cultivate, nurture, and enhance ecosystems for mutual abundance. Care for that which nourishes and drives productivity: water in all forms, soil fertility and nutrients, areas and seasons for reproduction. Continue to give to the *ʻāina* and learn from the *ʻāina*. Be on the *ʻāina*. Learn and practice ceremonies. Maintain a diversity of governance systems attuned to the diversity of ecosystems within and between re-gions. Revere resources, not as trees or water or forest to be extracted or even managed, but as the sources that feed and shape us, as embodiments of our gods, extensions and ancestors of us all. And continue to innovate and work for the sustained health and thriving of all that live in these islands.

4

Rapa Nui (Easter Island) Rock Gardens

Christopher M. Stevenson, Elisabeth S. V. Burns,
Sonia Haoa, Everett Carpenter, Caitlin S. M. Hunt,
Oliver A. Chadwick, and Thegn N. Ladefoged

Rapa Nui is a volcanic island like the Hawaiian Islands, it is isolated like Hawai'i, and it was discovered by Polynesian navigators fairly recently, again like Hawai'i. Rapa Nui differs from Hawai'i in that it is much smaller, about 1 percent of the land area (figure 4.1), and except in the lowlands, its soils on the whole are less fertile than those where agriculture was intensified in Hawai'i. The low fertility of Rapa Nui soils is due to relatively high, but also highly variable, rainfall. This rainfall variability means that there are times of prolonged drought that affect food production as well as times during which large quantities of water leach through the soil, which drives the weathering of minerals and the depletion of nutrients in the volcanic soils. Owing to the porous nature of the soils and substrates, there are no permanent streams on Rapa Nui, and there has been no opportunity

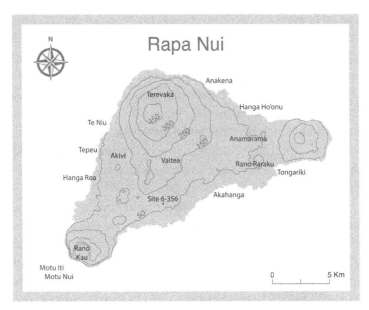

Figure 4.1. Map of Rapa Nui showing locations mentioned in the text. Contour lines are at 100-meter intervals, starting with 50 meters.

to develop flooded agricultural pondfields, or paddies (*lo'i*), as exist in Hawai'i and elsewhere.

Rapanui, the Indigenous people of Rapa Nui, are often depicted as the destroyers of their island's environment. Some writers believe that in their rush to feed their ever-growing population, and at the same time produce food surpluses to support people who were not producing food full-time—including those constructing statues and ceremonial platforms—they spurred vegetation clearance, erosion, and severe environmental degradation, which led to a "societal collapse." Although there is no compelling evidence for societal collapse before European contact, forest removal and a reduction of plant diversity certainly occurred. The loss of forests on Rapa Nui may have been caused by seed predation by rats that accompanied the discoverers; in Hawai'i the dramatic compositional change to forests that came about just after Polynesian discovery often occurred before the activities of people reached particular places. The loss of forest on Rapa Nui was associated with changes in the environment that may have included soil degradation driven in part by nutrient depletion by agriculture, and perhaps also by erosion associated with agriculture, although severe erosion is constrained spatially; in turn, soil degradation could have reduced agricultural production.

Despite these environmental transformations, Rapanui never experienced overall agrarian failure, although there is evidence for agricultural abandonment in marginal lands, abandonment which could have led to a decline in overall food production; rather, Rapanui sustained their productive systems in fertile lowland areas through early European contact and developed innovative agricultural techniques that allowed for sustained production elsewhere. These techniques included rock-walled gardens (*manavai*), stone-circled planting pits, and rock gardens with lithic mulch and stacked alignments. The rock gardens were invented in the fifteenth century and occurred in three principal forms: (A) with lithic mulch worked into the top 20–25 centimeters of the soil profile, (B) with a closely spaced veneer of fist-size rocks resting on the surface, and (C) with a distribution of boulders and intervening small stones (figure 4.2). The construction of these features created new niches for agricultural production, which fundamentally changed the relationships between people, cultigens and other plants, microbes, and nutrient cycling and enabled Rapanui to flourish in the face of a limited resource base.

The geochemical dynamics of Rapa Nui soils were integral for the successful production of crops and for surplus yields that could feed people other than full-time cultivators. Volcanic

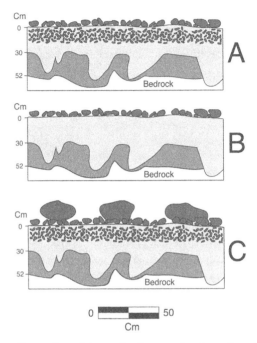

Figure 4.2. Examples of the major forms of rock gardens found on Rapa Nui, including (A) lithic mulch gardens, (B) veneer gardens, and (C) boulder gardens.

basalt is frequently credited with enhancing soils through the dissolution and release of plant-available nutrients crucial to the maintenance of agricultural productivity. As described in the chapter on Hawai'i, rain-fed agriculture there involved planting crops in areas where rock was breaking down naturally and supplying nutrients that crops could use. On Rapa Nui, could people have in effect reversed this process and brought little-weathered rocks to crops, to the widespread rock gardens in particular? A number of studies have documented that higher levels of soil nutrients that support plant growth are present within rock gardens. With the exception of a study by S. C. Sherwood and colleagues, these studies lack supporting experimental evidence that mineral dissolution within these rocks contributes to the nutrient pool in rock gardens. Here we explore the possibility that Rapa Nui rock gardens enhanced soil fertility by causing the breakdown of rocks and release of plant nutrients, which made their production system more sustainable.

Development of Rapa Nui Agriculture

The archaeological and pollen-core record of Rapa Nui reflects a massive transformation of the island's ecology after settlement in the mid-thirteenth century; changes included land clearance and the extinction of many bird species. Excavations in the dune deposits at Anakena Beach revealed an abundance of bird bones from some 25 species, of which only one survives today. Sediment cores taken from crater lakes and carbon from terrestrial sediments enabled radiocarbon-dating of seeds from totora reeds and endocarps from a now extinct palm (*Paschalococos disperta*); these measurements clearly showed deforestation of the endemic palm forest that was effectively lost in the coastal region of Rapa Nui by 1450 and at higher elevations by 1650. An increased input of charcoal into Rano Raraku Crater Lake sediments was indicative of the role that fire played in landscape management and was dated to 1180–1290. This corresponds to a period of soil erosion and increased pollen levels of herbaceous species that replaced the previously dominant palm forest.

In 2003, A. Mieth and H. R. Bork proposed that food production in the early years of human settlement remained within 1–2 kilometers of the coast and that after 1500 the remaining forested volcanic peaks were replaced by gardens. A plant microfossil analysis carried out by M. Horrocks and J. A. Wozniak and described in 2008 identified a mixed-crop dryland production system at Te Niu (see figure 4.1) dominated by *uhi* (yam) and *kumara* (sweet potato) and supplemented by *taro* (taro) and *hue* (bottle gourd), all of which were introduced to Rapa Nui by its Polynesian discoverers. The distribution of plant remains supports the indirect evidence that a substantial fraction of the rocky landscape of Rapa Nui was used for extensive agricultural production, despite low-fertility soils, although the permanence of these gardens is difficult to know. Shifting cultivation, in which resources are concentrated during a long fallow period and then utilized in a comparatively brief cropping period, no doubt was carried out on Rapa Nui (as elsewhere in Polynesia). Shifting cultivation is a sustainable system as long as the lengths of fallow periods are sufficient; however, shifting cultivation uses land inefficiently (compared to continuous cultivation), and it is difficult to produce a surplus that can support people who do not spend most of their time producing food with shifting cultivation. Alternatively, Rapanui cultivators could have met the constraints imposed by their environment by developing their innovative rock garden systems in otherwise low-fertility landscapes. They probably utilized both intensive rock gardens and extensive shifting cultivation. Thegn Ladefoged and colleagues' archaeological survey using high-resolution remotely sensed data suggested that between 2.5 and 12.7 percent of the island was used for agricultural rock gardens, while areas that remained without physical infrastructure were on old geological substrates and elevations above approximately 350 meters.

These rock gardens were innovative agricultural adaptations to environmental limitations. The lithic mulch aided in moisture retention, protected against wind erosion, and moderated soil temperature fluctuations. Wind protection was further achieved by stacked boulder concentrations. It has been suggested that lithic mulch gardens were used for shallow-

rooted crops such as *kumara,* while simple stone-covered surfaces and boulder gardens were used for *taro* and *uhi,* which
required deep planting pits for successful propagation.

Agriculture inherently involves the removal of essential
plant nutrients from agricultural systems, and the more productive the agricultural system, the greater the removal of nutrients.
Nitrogen and phosphorus are the elements that typically most
constrain soil fertility and the maintenance of long-term agriculture. Phosphorus is derived primarily from the breakdown
of rock, while nitrogen is largely supplied by biological nitrogen
fixation (which is enhanced by phosphorus supply). Continuous
gardening therefore requires regular nutrient (especially nitrogen
and phosphorus) amendments to be sustainable in the long term.
Soil fertility studies on Rapa Nui have analyzed the distribution
of nutrients across the island landscape and within the boundaries of agricultural systems. In 2005, based on limited sampling
in inland Vaitea, Ladefoged and colleagues proposed that low-
nutrient soils were relatively old geologic substrates with sustained depletion of nutrients by rainfall. They noted that rock
gardening might have been one way of enhancing nutrient levels of poor soils. In 2006, G. Louwagie and colleagues examined
four land units in the areas of Akivi, Vaitea, Akahanga, and La
Perouse (Hanga Ho'onu). This broad overview considered multiple factors, including temperature variability, soil depth and
drainage, and seasonal variation in rainfall, that all contributed
to making Rapa Nui a difficult place to farm. Soil analysis identified limiting factors, including depleted nutrient availability
due to andic (volcanic) soil properties and relatively high average rainfall, which caused low levels of phosphorus and potassium. The beneficial effects of lithic mulch gardens were
considered one component of a successful farming strategy, but
mineral enrichment through basalt dissolution was not considered as a potential solution to generally poor soil quality.

This study was followed in 2010 by a report on the investigations of Ladefoged and colleagues, who made two important contributions to the understanding of variations in soil fertility across the Rapa Nui landscape. First, a cross-island, coast-to-coast transect over the central volcano of Maunga Terevaka (elevation: 503 meters) was sampled at 250-meter intervals for soil-base saturation. An integrated measure of soil fertility, soil-base saturation is the proportion of negatively charged exchange sites in the soil matrix that are occupied by the non-hydrolyzing cations calcium, magnesium, potassium, and sodium—the first three of which are essential plant nutrients. Measurements showed a decline with elevation, which was inferred to be caused by higher rates of leaching over the millennia because of greater orographic rainfall at higher elevations. Second, soil samples taken from within and outside of rock gardens in the Te Niu (west coast) and Hanga Hoʻonu (north coast) regions of Rapa Nui documented that in all but one case, base saturation levels were higher within rock gardens than in the surrounding non-intensified areas. It was hypothesized that farmers may have sought out naturally occurring nutrient-rich "sweet spots" at the edges of weathered basalt outcrops. It was also suggested that rock fragmentation during garden construction may have accelerated mineral weathering, thereby increasing the nutrient levels of the relatively old volcanic substrates.

In a similar study of rock gardens in the Anamarama region of Rapa Nui in 2014, Peter Vitousek and colleagues established a 145-meter transect of short-interval samples that started in shallow soils at the base of a basalt outcrop and passed over two adjacent rock gardens and an area between them without agricultural infrastructure. Exchangeable calcium levels in the rock gardens were higher in each case ($\sim$9–11.8 mEq/100g) when compared to levels in the intervening non-garden areas ($\sim$5–9 mEq/100g). The calcium concentrations in rock gardens are close to those at the low-fertility (high-rainfall) boundary of an intensively cultivated agricultural field system in Hawai'i, while the levels in non-garden areas are below those where cultivators in Hawai'i established and maintained intensive agricultural field systems.

Mineral Fertilizers for Agriculture

The incorporation of intact rocks in crop production systems is believed to increase crop biomass and yield through several pathways. Rocks enhance moisture retention in soils by decreasing surface evaporation rates and increasing water infiltration. Soil temperature variation also is ameliorated by the absorption of solar energy. Additionally, rocks slow the velocity of erosive winds. Using rocks this way is not unique to Rapa Nui; it is also seen in Aotearoa (New Zealand), where shell, rock, and charcoal additives were mixed to create friable and nutrient-enriched soils, and by the Rio Grande Anasazi of northern New Mexico, who use pebble-mulch gardening primarily as a drought-avoiding measure to increase soil moisture, reduce erosion, moderate soil temperature, and increase crop yields. The use of rock and sand mulch was also a traditional practice in the arid loess plateau region of China.

It has been suggested that rock gardens on Rapa Nui also functioned to enhance soil nutrient levels through weathering of the relatively soft and porous basaltic rock. In a book written over 125 years ago, Julius Hensel suggested that the nutrient levels of depleted soils can be restored through the addition of "untouched earthy material" in the form of pulverized rocks. Here, we evaluate the potential effectiveness of this strategy for past Rapa Nui farming.

Calcium and magnesium make up about 5–7 percent and 3–6 percent by mass, respectively, of Rapa Nui lavas. Potassium and phosphorus each make up less than 0.7 percent of the lavas. These elements are hosted in relatively soluble primary minerals such as volcanic glass, plagioclase, and apatite. In soils these minerals come into contact with dissolved organic acids and carbonic acid, which drive mineral weathering and the release of elements into forms that can be used by plants. Weathering is enhanced by high surface to volume ratios of the minerals, which allow water and acids access to individual mineral surfaces. As a consequence, large rocks weather slowly, whereas finely divided volcanic material such as tephra weathers rapidly. Hence, fertilization with rock requires relatively fine-grained material to support nutrient release rates that would be meaningful over time frames of a few years and therefore useful for Rapa Nui farmers. On Rapa Nui, cinder cone deposits or crushed rocks from lava flows could provide such material.

In this chapter, we describe experiments that were designed to evaluate the possibility that one of the benefits of the rock gardens established by Rapanui cultivators could have been the enhancement of nutrient supply in low-fertility soils, thereby creating enriched sites in which intensive agriculture could be practiced sustainably.

Previous Experiments

Earlier studies into the fertilizing potential of basalt evaluated the biological availability of rock-derived mineral nutrients in aqueous solutions, and the results provided supporting evidence for the benefits of stone-mulching techniques. For example, a 2014 study by C. G. Ramos and colleagues found that all samples of volcanic rock that they tested released macro- and micronutrients essential to plant growth; they specifically identified the presence of calcium and magnesium, high alkalinity, good availability of phosphorus, an availability of potassium, and the presence of micronutrients such as zinc, boron, copper, iron, and manganese derived from volcanic rock.

Another experiment published in 2014, by J. M. G. Nunes and colleagues, identified the availability of the plant macro- and micronutrients calcium, magnesium, manganese, phosphorus, potassium, boron, and sulfur from acid volcanic rocks in aqueous solutions. The levels of macro- and micronutrients were found suitable for plant productivity with phosphorus being measured above 100 milligrams per liter (mg/L), potassium at 59–152 mg/L, sulfur at 1.8 mg/L, copper at 2.2–8.4 mg/L, manganese at 2–6 mg/L, and zinc at 1.6–1.8 mg/L.

In an extensive laboratory study in 2014, O. M. M. Lopes and colleagues applied basalt powder to two soil types (clayey and sandy) while testing pH as well as concentrations of soluble calcium (Ca^{2+}), magnesium (Mg^{2+}), and potassium (K^+). In clayey soil, there was a significant increase of Ca^{2+}, Mg^{2+}, and K^+ proportional to the rate of applied basalt powder. In sandy soil, there was an increase in Mg^{2+}, but Ca^{2+} remained at a statistically equal concentration, and K^+ decreased with all treatments. Most important, it was discovered that the pH of the soil solution was the main factor determining weathering rates of the applied powders.

In an earlier (2009) experiment, M. Anda and colleagues observed the effect of soil pH on cation exchange capacity and basalt application for cocoa growth. They determined that ground basalt continuously raised soil pH to more basic levels with increasing application rates. Furthermore, base cations were continuously released from the basalt and resulted in significantly enhanced levels of calcium, magnesium, potassium, and sodium both in forms of exchangeable cations and in soluble cations; there was an associated suppression of toxic elements such as aluminum. Their conclusion was that ground basalt soil amendments significantly improved cocoa growth.

Although it is convincing that basalt mineral fertilizers can have a positive effect on soil nutrients, could this process have been important in precolonial Rapa Nui? Rock gardens clearly improved growing conditions by providing an environmental buffer that reduced moisture stress, but we do not know whether more finely divided rock fertilizers also were applied. While the basaltic rocks of Rapa Nui are sufficiently mineral rich, and a number of spatially expansive soil-sampling and nutrient analyses on Rapa Nui have revealed that nutrient levels were enhanced within rock garden settings, we do not know if rock gardens (deliberately or not) enhanced basalt weathering, and we need to carry out experiments in order to explore this possibility. An alternative is that Rapanui selected already nutrient-rich sites.

Laboratory Methods

We tested the possibility that one of the benefits of rock gardens could have been enhanced soil fertility. We did so by grinding Rapa Nui basalt and leaching the resulting powder with water of similar acidity to that found on Rapa Nui. This test was designed to determine if rocks could have provided a source of important plant nutrients. To increase the chances of observing an effect (if one was there), we used powdered rock. We also used higher temperatures (50–90°C) than occur on Rapa Nui to accelerate the dissolution process so that a determination could be made in weeks rather than years. The use of higher temperatures to accelerate a reaction is a common strategy in geochemistry and is reasonable as long as other parameters (e.g., pressure) affecting the reaction do not change. Accordingly, our hypothesis was that rock could enhance soil fertility. It should be noted the test was one-sided in the sense that if under these conditions we did not observe an increased

availability of rock-derived nutrient elements, we would con-
clude that Rapanui cultivators would not have observed such
an effect in an agriculturally meaningful time frame with
larger pieces of rock and lower temperatures. If we did observe
an effect under our experimental conditions, further work
would be needed to see if this effect remained important with
larger rock fragments and/or lower temperatures.

The parent rock utilized as a source of basaltic powder
was a sub-rounded cobble, measuring 9.5 by 5 by 4 centimeters
and 204.89 grams, collected from the surface of an archaeological habitation site surrounded by rock gardens on the
southwestern section of Rapa Nui in 1988. This site is situated
on a lava flow originating from Terevaka eruptive fissures that
consist of hawaiites, olivine basalts, and mugearites. The collection site is mapped specifically to a hawaiite lava flow, but
because the rock is a portable cultural artifact, its geological
origin is not certain. Samples were cut from the basalt cobble
with a circular saw lubricated by water. Four 3-millimeter-thick
slabs were produced. The slabs were ground into a coarse powder using a porcelain mortar and pestle. The resulting coarse
material was sifted to produce a powder of 150 microns or less
in diameter.

To approximate Rapa Nui soil and rainwater conditions
at the site (soil pH measuring at 5.8–6.3 and rainwater pH at
6.3), a slightly acidic solution consisting of a mixture of am-
monium acetate and glacial acetic acid with a measured pH of
6.28 was created. This solution differed from rainwater (but was
similar to soils) in that its acidity was buffered, so that weathering will not rapidly change the acidity of the solution. Ten
1-gram samples of basalt powder were placed in individual
100-milliliter Chemware Teflon canisters. Forty milliliters of
the solution was added to each canister. The canisters were then
placed into four Quincy Lab Model 12-140 incubators set to

50°C, 60°C, 70°C, and 80°C. Additionally, a Thermo Scientific Heratherm Oven with mechanical convection was used as the fifth oven and set to 90°C.

Two sample canisters were placed in each of the five ovens with varying temperatures. After observing difficulties in stabilizing temperatures in the four Quincy Lab incubators, all eight prospective samples were removed approximately nine days (211 hours) after their initial placement and transferred into four Thermo Scientific Heratherm mechanical convection ovens set to the initial four temperature conditions. After a total duration of approximately six weeks (44 days, 19 hours, 40 minutes), half of the samples, one sample canister per oven, were removed from their ovens for analysis. The solution-phase samples were measured for concentration of essential plant elements and abundant constituents of Rapa Nui basalt (specifically, aluminum, boron, calcium, copper, iron, potassium, magnesium, manganese, phosporus, sulfur, silicon, and zinc) utilizing inductively coupled plasma optical emission spectroscopy (ICP-OES). The results are semi-semiquantitative, since only a single analytical standard was used (table 4.1).

Experimental Results

The ICP-OES method identified ten of the elements of interest in the solution phase of the incubations. Elevated amounts of calcium (18 ppm [parts per million]) and magnesium (23 ppm) were solubilized from basalt powder at 90°C; concentrations declined gradually as temperature decreased. The concentration of potassium remained relatively unchanged at 4 ppm across the 40-degree temperature range. In comparison, manganese and zinc were present in lower concentration (1.5 ppm at 90°C) and also varied with temperature. Iron was present in low concentrations in the solution phase and its temperature

Table 4.1.   Elemental Analysis of Leachate Solutions for Selected Plant Nutrients and Abundant Constituents of Rapa Nui Basalt (ppm)

Temperature	Al	B	Ca	Cu	Fe	K	Mg	Mn	Si	Zn
Standard*	0.05	0.16	0.09	0.08		0.02		1.15	0.08	
50°C	13.48	0.26	13.42	0.53	0.89	4.07	21.06	0.58	9.94	0.45
60°C	8.36	0.30	12.85	0.54	0.76	4.09	21.01	0.61	7.45	0.46
70°C	2.84	0.44	13.62	0.52	0.63	4.06	21.11	0.79	5.25	0.49
80°C	1.59	0.40	14.56	0.52	0.75	4.20	21.50	0.93	5.45	0.56
90°C	1.23	0.48	18.17	0.37	0.93	4.17	23.45	1.30	7.21	0.54

* A solution containing known quantities of elements, against which analyses of the samples are compared.

response varied in a less predictable fashion. Another unanticipated observation was the exponential increase in aluminum (1.23 to 13.28) as temperature declined from 90°C to 50°C. It is possible that the higher temperatures favored more rapid precipitation rates, hence depleting the aluminum in solution more rapidly. The biologically important element phosphorus was not detected during this analysis.

Discussion

When trying to understand the history of the Rapanui people, we are faced with addressing the "Rapa Nui enigma": How did pre-Contact farmers produce a consistent year-to-year food surplus on an island with marginal soils? One possibility is that a mixed strategy of rock garden technology, land-use planning, and systematic supervision may have helped raise yields on a consistent basis.

Our results indicate that under experimental conditions Rapa Nui basalt could break down and add nutritionally important elements to the soil. In conducting the experiment, we assumed that the experimental conditions of higher temperatures for shorter time periods were a good proxy for the real conditions that Rapanui experienced of lower temperatures for longer time periods. The next step would be longer-term experiments designed to determine the extent to which the possibility of nutrient enrichment could have been realized in practice.

A large number of gardens on Rapa Nui included a layer of compacted stone fragments 10–15 centimeters thick, referred to as lithic mulch (see figure 4.2). These stones may have been sourced from adjacent areas or brought to the surface from the lower regolith as planting pits were excavated into the subsoil. It has been suggested that these smaller and partially decomposed fist-sized rocks would have been the source of elemental addition. However, the surface area to volume ratio of these rocks is so low that dissolution rates would have been infinitesimal during a person's life span. Possibly Rapa Nui cultivators were acting for the benefit of future generations of cultivators. Alternatively, if mineral fertilization was to be effective during an individual cultivator's lifetime, how did accelerated weathering take place?

A higher ratio of surface area to volume is needed for enhanced mineral weathering, and it seems likely that it was not the smaller fist-sized rocks themselves but rather their alteration by the farming technology that represented the source of accelerated weathering and enhanced soil fertility. Precolonial agriculture on Rapa Nui was practiced with wooden digging sticks and hard-basalt hand hoes. Excavation through the lithic mulch layer to the softer soil below is difficult and requires repeated impacts to loosen the compacted rock fragments. This process of excavating planting pits through the lithic mulch cap would have occurred at the installation of a new planting pit and again at harvest time, when the surrounding rocks were removed, in each case generating some finer basalt particles.

Thousands of such planting and harvesting events in a garden could create a substantial amount of small particles. Farming in veneer gardens and boulder gardens would not have created small particles, because the surface stones were easily removed by hand prior to cultivation.

We should also consider the possibility that mineral powders were added to gardens for the purpose of generating nutrient enhancements. Rapa Nui farmers would not have had direct knowledge of nutrients; their characterization is a recent phenomenon globally and involved technology that Rapa Nui cultivators did not have. Nevertheless, they could have observed that crops were healthier and cropping was sustainable when powdered rock was added to soils, and used that practice to support their agriculture. Pulverized rock could have been derived from the debris generated by the shaping of basalt stones for house foundations and ceremonial platforms. Fine waste powders were also created by shaping statues with dense basalt picks obtained from quarries in the Hanga Hoʻonu region on the north coast of Rapa Nui. Other sources of mineral fertilizer could have been the scoria deposits at Puna Pau, or the numerous other cinder cones distributed across the island, and tephra deposits such as the one at Anakena on the north coast. Sherwood and colleagues also suggested in 2019 that soil transport by humans was a mechanism responsible for garden enrichment, in this case using the nutrient-rich soils found within the Rano Raraku volcanic crater.

Conclusion

The possible implications of creating rock gardens are clear. Basalts contain essential minerals that are readily available as nutrient constituents that can dissolve from the rocks when particle sizes are small. Specifically, the nutrients we observe include calcium, magnesium, and potassium and micronutrients such as zinc, boron, copper, iron, and manganese. No increase in phosphorus mobilization was observed in this study, although it has occurred in other studies discussed here. Phosphorus is a key element in agriculture, especially in tropical and subtropical environments—not least because it enhances the supply of nitrogen through biological nitrogen fixation. Moreover, the key factor to weathering rates of basalt within soil is pH, and basalt additions raise soil pH, which in turn increases the cation exchange capacity and reduces the toxicity of elements such as aluminum. Our experimental results suggest that Rapanui were actively enhancing soil nutrients by constructing rock gardens throughout their island home. This innovation enabled the Rapanui to flourish and to sustain themselves in a dynamic and challenging environment and produced the agricultural surpluses necessary to support their exceptionally creative culture.

Acknowledgments

We thank Mary Gurnick of Richard Bland College for the use of the chemistry analytical laboratory and her preparation of the solutions used in the experiment. Funding for this project was provided by the Virginia Commonwealth University and the University of Auckland.

5

Tikopia

A 3,000-Year Journey toward Sustainability

Patrick V. Kirch

Tikopia, a Polynesian outlier in the southeastern Solomon Islands, is one of the most thoroughly documented of oceanic societies, thanks to the unparalleled ethnographic fieldwork of Raymond Firth. With a land area of just 4.6 square kilometers, Tikopia ranks among the smallest Polynesian tropical high islands, yet with a population density of about 242 persons per square kilometer, it has one of the highest demographic concentrations recorded under an Indigenous oceanic subsistence regime. The island's agricultural system is highly intensive, yet it lacks both irrigation and extensive short-fallow dryland field cultivation. Rather, in Tikopia the high population density is supported by arboriculture, or what has more recently come to be called agroforestry, bolstered by the genetic manipulation of certain crops to adapt them to an intensive "orchard garden" regime.

Firth's simile (in his 1936 book, *We, the Tikopia*) of Tikopia as a "hollow bowl, old, battered, and moss-grown, with a broken irregular rim, one side of which is very much gapped

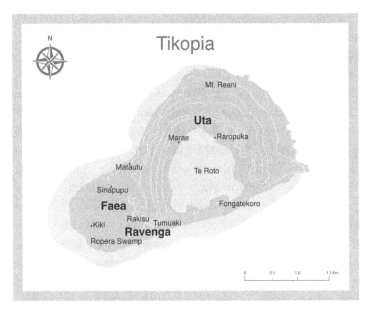

Figure 5.1. Map of Tikopia showing locations described in the text.

and the interior partially full of water" perfectly conjures an image of this eroded remnant of a Pleistocene volcano, the southern rim of which was blasted away in an explosive eruption, which permitted the sea to enter the former caldera. Development of a coral reef and a tombolo, or sand spit, across this sea gap converted the former bay to a brackish water lake, Te Roto (figure 5.1). The lake and its surrounding margins comprise the Ravenga district. In the lee of the volcanic cone, another reef flat about 1 kilometer wide was partially covered by an accretionary plain of calcareous sand and biogenic sediments, which lies between 1 and 4 meters above present sea level. This sandy plain, with fertile soils enriched by the addition of volcanic sediments eroded from the adjacent hillslopes, comprises the heavily populated core of the Faea district.

Three varied land systems make up the Tikopian landscape, each characterized by distinct associations of geomor-
phology, soil, vegetation, and human land use. The calcareous
lowlands (Lomousa Land System), found primarily in the Faea
district but also along the lake margins and on the Ravenga
tombolo, make up about 1.5 square kilometers. Small freshwater swamps at Ropera in Faea, and along the lake margin (0.1
square kilometers), are used for the cultivation of *pulaka* (giant
swamp taro, *Cyrtosperma chamissonis*); these constitute the
Pusuraghi Land System. The greatest part of the island, some
3.0 square kilometers, consists of volcanic slopes and ridges
classified as the Patukio Land System. Aside from these terrestrial resource zones, the Tikopia exploit both the lake and the
fringing reef (broadest along the southern, western, and northwestern coasts) for fish, shellfish, seaweed, and other lacustrine
and marine resources. Lacking domestic animals other than
chickens, the Tikopia depend almost entirely upon marine foods
for protein.

If viewed from the deck of one of the irregularly scheduled
small ships that are Tikopia's connection to the outer world, the
island's slopes appear to be cloaked in a typical rain-forest association from the shoreline right up to the summit of Reani,
the mountain peak. Protruding crowns of coconut palms that
break the canopy are the only hint that this "rain forest" is not a
natural forest at all but a highly productive, multistory mosaic
of orchard gardens. Exploration of the island's interior reveals
that virtually the entire terrestrial environment is an anthropogenic landscape. In Firth's words (again, from *We, the Tikopia*):
"As one wanders abroad, ascends the ring of hills that encircles
the lake, climbs the peak of Reani or skirts the rugged northern
shore, it becomes evident that the whole place is in a high state
of economic utilization, that gardens are made right up the
mountain, and that what appears to be bush is really a collection

of trees and shrubs, each having its own value to the people, either for its food or in their material arts." Only small tracts of nearly vertical cliff retain anything approaching natural vegetation. Owing to the island's extreme isolation—geographic, economic, and political—Tikopia has remained an essentially closed, or self-sustaining, production system, completely lacking cash cropping or commercialization of production.

While the classic oceanic root-crop complex of *taro* (*Colocasia esculenta*) and *uhi* (multiple species of *Dioscorea*, or yam) are important components of Tikopia subsistence— indeed, they are ritually its essence—it is perennial tree crops that dominate the agricultural landscape, lending a distinctive character to Tikopia agriculture. The key arboricultural taxa are *mei* (breadfruit, *Artocarpus altilis*), *ota* (sago palm, *Metroxylon salomonense*), and *niu* (coconut palm, *Cocos nucifera*), forming much of the artificial forest canopy, along with the fruit- and nut-producing *ifi* (Tahitian chestnut, *Inocarpus fagiferus*), *voia* (sea almond, *Canarium harveyi*), *vere* (cut nut, *Barringtonia procera*), *vi* (vi apple, *Spondias dulcis*), *kavariki* (tropical almond, *Terminalia catappa*), *kaula* (betel-nut palm, *Areca catechu*), and finally the barkcloth-yielding *mami* (upas, *Antiaris toxicaria*). The use of *Antiaris* as the source of bast for barkcloth, rather than the typical Polynesian paper mulberry (*Broussonetia papyrifera*), is a further reflection of this emphasis on agroforestry. When mature, *Antiaris* is a medium-sized tree and can be fully integrated into a mixed-species orchard garden. These trees are mixed in a multistory association shading a subcanopy of what are typically annual crops but which in Tikopia have been converted to perennial production, especially *pulaka* (giant swamp taro), but also *futi* (*Musa* sp., bananas), and *uhi* (multiple species of yams, *Dioscorea*). This complex, multistory system of orchard gardening is possibly unique in Oceania in the degree to which it mimics the structure of natural low-altitude forest ecosystems, both in tree species and in the subcanopy, representing an apogee in the adaptation and elaboration of agroforestry as one mode of agricultural intensification. All of the economic plants represent human introductions to Tikopia.

The adaptation of *pulaka* to this arboricultural regime is of special note, for it exemplifies a "genetic" mode of agricultural intensification. This large aroid, one of several domesticates of undoubted Island Southeast Asian origin, normally is short-lived and requires saturated soils, typified by its use in pit cultivation throughout atolls. In West Polynesia it is grown in swampy terrain on the margins of *taro* irrigation systems. While swamp cultivation of *pulaka* is also practiced on Tikopia (especially in the Ropera swamp and along the low lying hydromorphic margins of Te Roto lake), the plant's primary agricultural environment here is the steep, well-drained colluvial slopes and hillsides of the volcanic cone, where it is the dominant understory component of the orchard gardens and a perennial. This particular cultivar, called *pulaka vao*, is distinguished by the presence of numerous thorns on the petiole. While *pulaka* is not culturally or ritually significant, as are *taro* and *uhi* (yams), it contributes significantly to the overall caloric intake of most Tikopia.

While most of the island's arable land surface is cloaked in this multistory mosaic of permanent orchard gardens, there are a few areas of permanent short-fallow, rain-fed field cultivation; in aggregate these make up less than 10 percent of the cultivated land. The short-fallow open fields are devoted to a rotation of *taro* with manioc (*Manihot esculenta*). As a historic introduction of American origin, manioc has gained prominence in recent decades, largely replacing *uhi*'s role in rain-fed fields. The most important zone of rain-fed field cropping is at Rakisu, where it occupies a series of sloping colluvial fans at the base of the volcanic hill in Faea district. The Rakisu zone, about

0.56 kilometers long and varying from 40 to 120 meters wide, is divided into numerous small plots, marked by hedge rows. In contrast with the orchard gardens, cultivation of this zone requires constant labor input, primarily in weeding, mulching, and tending the *taro* and manioc crops. Rakisu, and smaller dry-field areas such as the summit of Tumuaki, are the only vestiges on Tikopia of what was probably once a more dominant cultivation mode, at an earlier phase in the island's agricultural history.

Three Millennia of Land Use on Tikopia

Tikopia was first settled between 2029–1769 cal B.P. (calendar years Before Present) by people embedded within the famous Lapita long-distance exchange network extending from the Bismarck Archipelago throughout the Solomon Islands. The oldest settlement site on Tikopia, which lends its name to the Kiki Phase (ca. 900–100 BCE—before the Common Era), contained such exotic artifacts as transported metavolcanic stone adzes, Talasea (New Britain) obsidian, and chert flakes, which testified to this Lapita linkage. A major cultural transition occurred about eight to ten centuries later (between about 100 BCE and 100 CE), marked archaeologically by the cessation of local plain pottery manufacture and by the importation of new kinds of artifacts—especially Mangaasi-style ceramics and Banks Islands obsidian from the Vanuatu archipelago to the south. For about 1,300 years, during what we have termed the Sinapupu Phase, Tikopia continued to maintain external connections with islands to the south. Then, between 1158 and 1212 CE, a major cultural transition is apparent, marked by the cessation of Mangaasi pottery imports and by the appearance of distinctly West Polynesian material culture traits (basalt adzes, two-piece trolling hooks, ornament styles, etc.). This transition

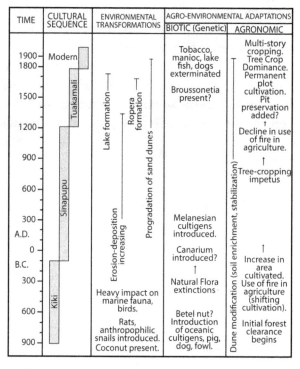

Figure 5.2. Summary chart of the Tikopia cultural and
environmental sequence, 900 BCE–1900 CE.

to the Tuakamali Phase (ca. 1200–1800) reflects the arrival
on Tikopia of new Polynesian-speaking immigrant groups
from West Polynesia, as attested also in richly detailed oral
traditions.

The main lines of evidence for changes in the island's
production system, inferred on the basis of varied strands of
evidence—geomorphological, faunal, paleoethnobotanical, and
artifactual—are summarized in figure 5.2. This chart indicates
the complexity of processes involved in the evolution of the

PRODUCTION SYSTEM TRANSFORMATIONS		PUTATIVE CULTURAL CHANGES	TIME
AGRICULTURE	HUNTING / FISHING		

Modern lineage system tapu incorporating elements of the developmental past.
Internal development of food tapu.
Internal modification of lineage system.
Lifting of food restriction.
Polynesian lineages.

Imposition of food restriction

Introduction of foreign lineage system

Tapu ⎱ Unknown
Lineage ⎰
systems

Local extinction of resource

Agriculture labels: Shifting cultivation; Arboriculture; Introduction of Santa cruz species; Animal husbandry; Fowl; Oceanic trees; Pigs, dogs, fowl

Hunting/Fishing labels: Fish; Sharks, rays absent; Megapode extinct; Wild birds; Turtles

Time axis: 1900, 1800, 1500, 1200, 900, 600, 300, A.D., 0, B.C., 300, 600, 900

island's production system, along with the lack of precise temporal correspondence to cultural phases.

The Lapita colonists who discovered Tikopia early in the first millennium BCE arrived on an island only about 72 percent the size of its modern configuration but with more extensive areas of undisturbed reefs, densely forested hills, and a diverse bird life. These colonists practiced a broad-spectrum horticultural-marine economy; they introduced pigs and chickens (the *Gallus gallus* fowl), along with the commensal Pacific rat (*Rattus exulans*). Dogs and a larger species of rat were introduced later in the Kiki

Phase, the latter possibly as a food source. The abundant fish and shellfish resources of the island were heavily exploited, as were land birds and seabirds, including larids, boobies, frigate birds, and the megapode, the last soon to be exterminated on the island.

At this early phase in the establishment of the island's agro-ecosystem, shifting cultivation—involving clearance of the natural climax rain forest and short-term farming—was the primary agricultural mode. An early use of fire in forest clearance is attested in the soil sections exposed by excavations in the Rakisu field system, where the deeper colluvial layers include charcoal flecking and lenses, indicating the use of fire in the agricultural system. Tikopian orchard gardening, as ethnographically attested, never uses fire, and the more recent upper soil layers in Rakisu exhibit a total absence of charcoal. This differential stratigraphic distribution of charcoal in the Rakisu sections is widespread and significant. The early use of fire in clearing and transforming the Tikopia terrestrial landscape and the later elimination of fire as a tool in the Tikopia gardening repertoire is one archaeologically detectable signal of a major shift in agronomic practice.

By the Sinapupu Phase, the Tikopia environment—both physical and biotic—had undergone considerable changes owing in part to natural processes but mostly reflecting nearly a millennium of human land use. The calcareous coastal beach ridges had prograded significantly, in part at least owing to human-caused erosion in the uplands. This erosion created more level land for settlement and for gardening. More dramatic were changes in the island's terrestrial fauna, including a significant decrease in the diversity and quantities of land and sea birds. Similar effects are evidenced for natural marine resources. Turtles, for example, had been heavily exploited in the earlier Kiki Phase, and the large nesting populations of marine turtles had been decimated.

This reduction in availability of wild food resources seems to have been offset by development of the island's agroecosystem. By about 500 CE, forest clearance using fire on the higher volcanic ridges had resulted in significant erosion and deposition of colluvial fan deposits at Rakisu, as is documented by excavations. The presence of at least one major tree crop, the *Canarium indicum* almond, is attested by carbonized endocarp remains dating to the beginning of the Sinapupu Phase, but whether the Tikopia agricultural system had begun its major transformation to agroforestry by this date is uncertain. However, the use of fire in gardening was soon to decline, indicated by the absence of charcoal in later sediments at Rakisu.

More substantive evidence of increased intensity of terrestrial production is provided by the faunal record, for pigs (*Sus scrofa*) are represented by an order of magnitude increase in Sinapupu Phase deposits. During this period, pigs accounted for about 45 percent of the total human protein intake from all vertebrates, including fish. This suggests a real emphasis on animal husbandry. Thus, the later elimination of pigs from the Tikopia production system is all the more startling.

During the Sinapupu Phase, the island was integrated into a long-distance exchange network that extended southward into the Banks Islands and northern Vanuatu and incorporated Vanikoro in the Santa Cruz group. The material evidence for this network in Tikopia consists of Mangaasi-style ceramics as well as Banks Islands obsidian, while a genomic memory of these contacts persists today in the presence of genetic markers in the modern Tikopia population. These southern connections may have contributed to the developing Tikopian production system through the acquisition of various new crop plants, such as *Metroxylon*, *Areca*, and other "Melanesian" tree crops, but also through cultural influences on the food system. The total absence of sharks, rays, and turtles from the faunal assemblage during the Sinapupu Phase cannot be explained by such factors as ecological disturbance or overexploitation or a sampling error of the archaeological record. Given the strong totemic associations of these marine species in ethnographically documented cultures throughout the southeast Solomons and Vanuatu, these marked absences in the archaeological faunal record likely signal a change in the island's symbolic food system. The reappearance of sharks, rays, and turtles in the archaeological record at the beginning of the Tuakamali Phase, which is associated with the arrival of Samoic-Outlier–speaking peoples on Tikopia, documents the replacement of one set of food restrictions with a different dietary code.

The arrival of Polynesian speakers around 1200 (and probably continuing, since more than one arrival is recorded in Tikopia oral traditions) involved both intermarriage with the local population and dominance of the island both culturally and linguistically. These arrivals set the stage for the Tikopia of Firth's "ethnographic present." It was during this final phase that we can most clearly resolve in the archaeological record the channeling of Tikopian agricultural development along an arboricultural pathway. The island's physiography continued to change after 1200, especially in the lowland and coastal regions. Continued progradation of the calcareous beach ridges led to a significant expansion of the Faea lowlands, and a concomitant seaward shift in village location opened up the core of the fertile Faea lands for agriculture. In Ravenga, a tombolo began to accrete on the narrow reef flat by about 1400, eventually closing off the connection between the old volcanic crater and the sea and forming the brackish lake Te Roto. This trans formation of Te Roto had dramatic consequences for marine resources, since the decreased salinity and circulation in the lake were fatal to the rich populations of sand-dwelling bivalves along the lake shores. The elimination of these shellfish beds, and of marine fish that would have formerly inhabited the embayment, was only partly offset by increases in the brackish-water *kiokio* fish (*Chanos chanos*). These environmental trans-formations were to have far-reaching implications for the island's human occupants by precipitating a series of inter-tribal wars over control of the island's prime agricultural lands, as recorded in both oral tradition and the archaeological record.

The major transformation from shifting cultivation to the orchard-gardening characteristic of Tikopian production in historic times appears to have occurred during the Tuakamali Phase. Carbonized fragments of the *Canarium* almond, one of the contemporary arboricultural dominants, become fairly common in archaeological deposits of the Tuakamali Phase. Although plant macrofossils are not plentiful in the Tikopia deposits, other finds from late prehistoric to protohistoric contexts included the fruits of cut nut and vi apple, coconut shell fragments, and part of the petiole of a sago palm, all com-ponents of the island's arboricultural crop roster.

Of particular note is the appearance of subterranean starch fermentation and storage pits. These *masi* pits, in which breadfruit and other farinaceous crops are stored for periods of up to two or three years, are an essential aspect of Tikopian subsistence economy, allowing for the storage and year-round distribution of staple starch. Because breadfruit, *Burckella*, and other tree crops of the Tikopia orchard-gardening system pro-duce high yields of temporally short duration, the *masi* pits confer an essential buffering of subsistence from the periodic vagaries of drought, cyclones, and food scarcity. *Masi* technol-ogy has been traced through archaeological evidence to the ancestral Polynesian phase in Tonga and Samoa; it appears to have become incorporated into the Tikopian production system only after the arrival of Polynesian immigrants in the Tuaka-mali Phase.

Perhaps the most dramatic of all changes in Tikopian production was the sudden elimination of pigs late in the Tuakamali Phase. This event—for indeed it seems to have been a calculated and abrupt act—is clearly signaled in archaeological faunal assemblages. It is also recorded in Tikopia oral tradition and in an early post-Contact account by the trader-explorer Peter Dillon. At Tikopia in 1827, Dillon observed that the island supported "neither hogs nor poultry," an obvious detriment to voyagers such as himself who required refreshment and resupply. Dillon continued, "They at one time had both, but they were voted common nuisances and exterminated by general consent. The hogs destroyed their plantations of yams, sweet potatoes, taras [taro], and bananas" (Vol. II, 1829, p. 134). Dillon's reporting of an Indigenous explanation for the absence of pigs was confirmed a century later by Firth, whose account (from his 1959 book, *Social Change in Tikopia*) follows: "In mid-June, 1952, when I was sitting in Kafika temple in Uta, chatting after a rite, I saw a pig jaw attached to the central post of the building; it was used to hang up a water bottle. On asking its origin, I was told it came from the time of Nga Ravenga (? about 1750). I queried this, . . . whereupon the Ariki Kafika replied that both Nga Ravenga and Nga Faea—ancestral sharers of the land with the progenitors of the present Tikopia—kept pigs." Firth also reports, like Dillon, that the pigs were destroyed "because of their depredations on the crops."

Population and Sustainability

Tikopia appears to be a model of a sustainable ecosystem, in terms of both the character of its production system and the emphasis of the society on stability of the human population. Yet with a population that hovers very close to the island's carrying capacity, sustainability has a cost, a cost measured in human lives unborn and human lives taken. According to Firth in 1936, the Tikopia themselves "realize the existence of a food problem in general as well as in individual terms. Not only is there a tendency for families to be regulated in size according to the quantity of their orchards and other ground, but there is a conception of a total population for which food has to be provided." The Tikopia express this concept as *fakatau ki te kai,* or "measured according to the food."

Firth's work on Tikopia demography amply documents the "mechanisms of population control" that were applied prior to the influx of European ideology. The catalogue of mechanisms (as he referred to them in his 1936 book, *We, the Tikopia*) includes celibacy, prevention of conception, abortion, infanticide, sea voyaging (generally suicidal) by young males, and ultimately the expulsion of some segment of the population. The traditional ritual cycle ("the work of the gods") encoded an ideology of zero population growth, annually proclaimed by the Ariki Tafua during the rites at Rarokoka. The *fono,* or proclamation at Rarokoka, included the following memorable exhortation of zero population growth, regulated by the arboricultural basis of the food supply (here quoted in Firth's 1967 book, *The Work of the Gods in Tikopia*):

> One male and one female
> That is the plucking of the coconut and the carrying of the water bottle
> The man who will persist in creating himself a family
> Where is his basis of trees he will create his family for?
> He will make a family merely to go and steal.

When, beginning in the 1920s, the Christian Mission prevented the application of the more stringent of these population control measures, the Tikopia population grew rapidly

from about 1,200 in 1929 to a peak of 1,753 in 1952. This 1952
peak exceeded the capacity of the production system to respond
to periodic environmental disasters. When cyclones struck in
February 1952 and again in March 1953 (damaging 50 percent
of the crops), famine ensued. Only the intercession of the
government in sending relief supplies—at the instigation of
anthropologist Firth—prevented wholesale death and the probability of social disintegration. Subsequently, the Tikopia resolved, at least for the time being, their population problem by
obtaining land grants on other islands of the Solomons group;
in 1976 as many Tikopia lived off-island as the 1,115 allowed by
the council of chiefs to live on the home island. The resident
population on Tikopia itself continues to be closely monitored
by the chiefs, who are acutely aware that their sustainable ecosystem depends upon a delicate balance between human numbers and productive resources.

Conclusions

The history of agriculture and production in Tikopia repeats
some trends that are widespread in Oceania. The heavy early
reliance on naturally occurring wild food resources such as birds,
fish, turtles, and shellfish and the dramatic reductions in populations of these resources due to human predation and predation
by animals introduced by humans are common to the histories
of many islands. So is the transformation of the natural flora
and vegetation patterns to anthropogenic mosaics, although the
degree of such floral transformation varies from island to island.
In Tikopia we have also the conscious elimination of pigs from
the production and food systems, a development also found in
some other islands, such as Mangaia and Mangareva.

Despite such trends in common, the Tikopia ultimately
created a distinctive agricultural landscape founded on intensive

arboriculture, or agroforestry. Through a particular combination of historical contingency, human choice, and environmental constraint and opportunity, the Tikopia gradually evolved a highly intensive multistory system of orchard gardening. Their agricultural history depended in part on the availability and genetic selection of particular cultivars, especially the *pulaka vao* clone of the giant swamp taro, which was adapted to hillslope planting. Technological innovations such as the use of *masi* fermentation pits and storage to confer temporal stability to food distribution were also critical components of this arboricultural strategy. In contrast to settlers on some other islands, the Tikopia made no use of permanent structural modifications to the agricultural landscape such as terraces or systems of water control. The deep-time history of agriculture in Tikopia reminds us that agricultural intensification has multiple pathways and that contingency is as significant as common cultural ancestry in influencing the flow of history.

One final lesson of the Tikopia case lies in the fundamental linkage between agricultural production and population, a link that is essential to the sustainability of this or any other social-environmental system. On this small island, where the connection between food supply and family size was readily evident, the Tikopia developed a moral code of zero population growth. "The plucking of the coconut and the carrying of the water bottle," one boy and one girl to replace their parents in the next generation, was the ideal reproductive strategy encoded in the *fono* of Rarokoka. Some of the means used to enforce this code appear draconian by Euro-American standards; when these practices were suppressed by Anglican missionaries in the twentieth century, the Tikopia population overshot the island's carrying capacity, resulting in famine and near disaster.

Acknowledgment

This chapter is based partly on chapter 12 of P. V. Kirch, *The Wet and the Dry: Irrigation and Agricultural Intensification in Polynesia* (Chicago: University of Chicago Press, 1994).

6

Mahinga kai nō Tonganui (New Zealand)

Making a Living in South Polynesia, 1250–1800

Atholl Anderson

South Polynesia comprises mainland New Zealand and its outlying archipelagoes, 600–900 kilometers distant, that were colonized from New Zealand: the Norfolk, Kermadec, Chatham, and Subantarctic Islands. The South Polynesians were Māori, originating in the Society Islands, who began to arrive in New Zealand by way of the Cook Islands, as recently as 750 or so years ago (about 1250–1300 CE). Their earliest recorded island names are Te Ika ā Maui, "Maui's fish," for the North Island and Te Wai Pounamu, "the land of jade," for the South Island (see figure 6.1). The name Aotearoa occurs in later traditional writings, usually to mean the North Island, but a tradition from northern New Zealand suggests that an earlier name for New Zealand as a whole was Tonganui, meaning "the big, south land."

The chapter title refers to the unremitting and indispensable activity of Māori, making food (*mahinga kai*). In discussing this topic, I emphasize several points. Most important are the ways in which South Polynesia was a distinct and different region from all of the rest of Polynesia through its location and biogeography. Both of those led to considerable regional variation in settlement patterns, with substantial early depletion of the natural resource landscape prominent to the south and late development of large-scale food production to the north. The regional differences in land use and population growth were sharpened by climate change, arising from the Little Ice Age and the asymmetrical resource landscape and population density distribution induced by rising levels of warfare and widespread internal migration.

The South Polynesian Region

Polynesians colonized the central Pacific islands in two distinct migrations that, in each case, placed a relatively large colonizing population in a new region in which settlement of an initial core area was followed by dispersal to all the habitable islands. About 1000–1200, migration from West Polynesia reached central East Polynesia (from Society to the Marquesas Islands), and then it continued into the East Polynesian margins, including Hawai'i and Rapa Nui. About 1280–1300, migration began again, now to the southwest, from central East Polynesia to New Zealand and then to the outlying islands of South Polynesia. To a small extent, contact and exchange were maintained between West Polynesia and parts of East Polynesia throughout the pre-European era, but South Polynesia appears to have been isolated, except during the initial migration period, when there might have been some return voyaging. If return voyaging did occur, it was probably seldom, both because New Zealand had a vastly greater landmass and diversity of resources than had been available in any of the central East Polynesian islands and also because, as the migration traditions recount in detail, the people who reached New Zealand had been effectively exiled. Early East Polynesian artifacts have been found in early New Zealand archaeological sites, but nothing of South Polynesian provenance, such as artifacts of New Zealand basalt, metamorphosed argillite, silcrete, porcellanite, flint, jade, or moa bone, has been found archaeologically in East Polynesian sites.

The relatively sharp boundary between East and South Polynesia was not just a matter of distance and social rupture, but also a matter of migration from one mode of oceanic cultural ecology, in which Polynesian ancestors had several thousand years' experience, to another that was quite new and radically different. How different can be epitomized by the distribution of the combined East and South Polynesian landmass and the eighteenth-century population. South Polynesia had 94 percent of the landmass but only 20–25 percent of the population of East and South Polynesia together, whereas East Polynesia had 75–80 percent of the population on only 6 percent of the land. Implicit in this difference are fundamental ecological reasons for the diverging cultural trajectories.

First and foremost, South Polynesia extends latitudinally from the subtropical Norfolk and Raoul Islands at 29° south to the subpolar Auckland Islands at 51° south, and its situation near the middle of the southern (ocean-dominated) hemisphere is reflected in cooler temperatures for latitude than in the northern hemisphere or even along continental margins in the south. Mainland New Zealand is in the temperate zone and has mean annual temperatures at the coast of 15°C in Auckland and 11°C in Dunedin, compared to 21°C and 24°C in subtropical Easter Island and Hawai'i (respectively) and 26°C in tropical Tahiti. The New Zealand climate is dominated by mid-latitude

New Zealand

Bay of Islands

• Pourerua
NORTHLAND

Kaipara Harbour ——

Coromandel

Tamaki
• Mayor Island
AUCKLAND

Te Ika ā Maui
(North Island)

WAIKATO
EAST COAST

TARANAKI
Hawkes Bay

Golden Bay
Marlborough
Sounds

WELLINGTON

Tasman Bay ——
—— Cook Strait

• Kaikoura

Banks Peninsula

OTAGO
• Shag River

Te Wai Pounamu
(South Island)

Figure 6.1. Map of New Zealand showing areas and places
mentioned in the text.

westerlies and a constant succession of cyclonic and anticy-clonic systems at intervals of a week or less.

Second, nearly all the land of South Polynesia was con-centrated in mainland New Zealand (268,000 square kilome-ters), with less than 2,000 square kilometers in all other islands combined. The two main islands of New Zealand are very large by Polynesian standards and almost ten times the size of the Hawaiian Islands, the next largest group. On a map of the east-ern United States, New Zealand would reach from the Cana-dian border to Cape Hatteras and cover all the land area of New England plus the eastern half of New York and south to Mary-land (figure 6.1).

Third, while East Polynesian islands are largely built from basalt and coral limestone, the New Zealand islands are geo-logically continental, with areas of recent volcanic activity in the north. The varied lithology and soils supported tall forests of Gondwanan origin and a terrestrial fauna that evolved in the absence of mammalian predators and included numerous flightless birds, notably nine species of the giant *moa* (moa, Dinornithiformes). Marine mammals, especially seals, and colony-nesting marine birds, notably petrels, shearwaters, penguins, and albatrosses, inhabited the coasts.

MIGRATING TO SOUTH POLYNESIA

Virtually the whole of East and South Polynesia was colonized within a period of 200–300 years in an extremely rapid and extensive burst of migration. This might be seen as exemplify-ing the ecological imperative of continual movement of mi-grants at low population densities in order to maintain high levels of resource access. In other words, the early colonists would move often because they were intolerant of a decline in their expected standards of living. In such circumstances, the outward thrust of voyaging could be expected to overshadow any countermovement back to areas of origin. This seems to be the case in South Polynesia especially. Not only was there very limited contact with East Polynesia after the canoe migrations ceased in the late fourteenth century, but there was also no evident interaction between New Zealand and its outlying islands. Māori carried and discarded Mayor Island (New Zealand) obsidian during initial occupation of the outlying islands, but there is neither archaeological evidence nor tradition to indicate return voyaging.

Why South Polynesia should be so different from East Polynesia in this respect also raises the issue of seafaring capability. Sailing in the westerlies was certainly challenging. Prevailing easterlies (trade winds) in the tropical Pacific tend to be steady and dry under clear skies, but the westerlies are disturbed, strong, and often cloudy. Annual average tropical wind speeds are less than 10 kilometers per hour, but in the westerlies they are 27 kilometers per hour at 40° south and over 50 kilometers per hour at 50° south. Nevertheless, modern Polynesian-style voyaging canoes have made numerous passages in those conditions to and within South Polynesia.

The more critical issue, as I explained in 2017 in the *Journal of the Royal Society of New Zealand,* is that archaeological and historical evidence indicates that the oceanic spritsail, commonly regarded as the ancestral Polynesian rig and used now in experimental voyaging, did not develop until after 1500 and did not reach New Zealand until about 1826. Earlier sailing, including during the periods of East and South Polynesian migration, used the double spritsail, an ancient Austronesian rig that survived up to the early nineteenth century in New Zealand. As that was basically a running sail, canoes had no windward ability and were significantly limited in sailing direction, sailing season, and passage speed, which often meant long periods at sea to reach distant destinations. With lighter winds and in more predictable tropical conditions, a level of maritime interaction with numerous islands was feasible, but in the heavy, unpredictable conditions of the mid-latitudes, with few and widely dispersed islands, the costs of distant voyaging may have been too high to sustain for long.

In addition, there was a major shift in South Pacific wind directions during the pre-European era. Research on decadal variation of pressure systems and wind patterns has shown that westerlies were largely replaced by easterly winds during the twelfth to mid-fourteenth centuries and in the mid-fifteenth century. With prevailing easterlies, migratory canoes could sail steadily downwind to South Polynesia under the double sprit-sail. Māori traditions indicate that our ancestors arrived in 12–20 colonizing canoes over a migration period lasting up to the fifteenth century. Westerly wind dominance then resumed over South Polynesia up to the modern era.

It is widely assumed, largely in the absence of specific evidence, that Polynesians embarked on deliberate colonization passages, taking with them all that they needed, including their garden plants and domestic animals. Transport of this "portmanteau biota" could have occurred in much of East Polynesia, although the failure of one or more pigs, dogs, rats, and chickens to reach (or to persist in) some marginal islands, such as Rapa Nui, indicates that it was not universally successful. In South Polynesia it was even less so. Only the dog and the Pacific rat (*Rattus exulans*) reached New Zealand, and only the dog reached the Auckland Islands. The Kermadecs, Norfolk Island, and the Chathams had only the rat.

Plant distribution is more difficult to document, but there is no sign archaeologically or in sedimentary coring of any cultivation in the Norfolk, Kermadec, or Chatham Islands, and the Aucklands were certainly too cold to support tropical cultigens.

In New Zealand there is coring evidence of *taro* (taro) pollen dating to 1425, but Bay of Plenty Māori traditions say that *hue* (gourd) was introduced long before *taro* and *kumara* (sweet potato), and Taranaki Māori traditions say that *taro* came relatively late. Canoe traditions about *kumara,* by far the main cultigen in New Zealand, are detailed but contradictory. Nevertheless, there is a tradition shared by several northern *iwi* (tribes) that *kumara* was unknown in the tropical homeland at the time of migration to New Zealand, that some tubers were later brought to New Zealand, and that planting stock was obtained by voyaging back to East Polynesia. These points suggest that while the portmanteau biota model of transferring plants and animals in Polynesia might have some currency in East Polynesia, it has little in South Polynesia, where the process was haphazard, as with introduced animals, and protracted. The archaeological chronology of *kumara* arrival is a particular case in point.

    Kumara (sweet potato) cultivation in marginal East Polynesia does not seem to have begun before the fifteenth century, and now that the age of *kumara* arrival, as delimited by radiocarbon ages at Tangatatau in Mangaia, has been lifted to about 1400, it remains to be seen whether convincing evidence of earlier *kumara* cultivation can be adduced elsewhere in central East Polynesia. In regard to South Polynesia, key radiocarbon ages supporting the arrival of *kumara* in New Zealand by 1150–1300 are derived from charcoals from unidentified or long-lived taxa, raising issues of inbuilt age (the problem that radiocarbon dating may determine when tissue was produced rather than when a particular cultural event occurred), in particular through the incorporation of charcoal from burnt ancient forest trees in preparing areas for cultivation. There are thus questions also about the clarity of chronological associations between garden features and charcoal samples. Similar problems attend the use of *kumara* microfossils, such as starch grains, which are highly mobile stratigraphically, to determine contemporaneity with radiocarbon ages on other materials. However, in recent projects in Coromandel, Waikato, and Tasman Bay, where radiocarbon samples are from charcoal samples of short-lived taxa or from associated marine shells, and where samples have been taken from within garden structures apparently specifically used in *kumara* cultivation and seemingly undamaged since their time of use, the results give dates exclusively before 1400.

There was, of course, gardening in New Zealand earlier than that, but presumably for *taro*, *hue* (bottle gourd), and *uhi* (yam). The numerous in-ground storage pits, required by the seasonality of gardening in New Zealand, are often assumed to have been for *kumara* storage, but ethnographic data indicate that while they were often for *kumara,* they had many uses, including storage of *taro, uhi, ti* (*Cordyline* root), seeds, and berries.

DIVIDING THE LAND

While East and South Polynesia had different patterns of maritime mobility and interaction, their colonists had a more or less common understanding about the origins of their new lands and how they were to be socially constructed for settlement. Islands did not emerge over the horizon into the gaze of the hopeful seafarer. They existed first as fish. Deities and culture heroes, to which Polynesian populations traced their genealogies, traveled about the ocean, caught the fish, and, in the course of subduing the piscine struggles, slashed and bludgeoned them into the broad shapes of the island topographies. New Zealand's Te Ika ā Maui was cognate with Tahiti and Mangaia, which were each visualized as fish of the deity Rongo swimming away from the afterworld in the west and into the currents of the easterly trade winds toward the life-giving sunrise.

The newly discovered lands were divided territorially in ways connected closely to the status relationships of chiefdoms. In traditionally ramified Polynesian societies, genealogical proximity to the main line of the clan or tribal ancestor ranked each person, family, or clan in a scale of seniority; in Māori society, every relationship is either with *tuākana* (senior) or *tēina* (junior) persons or groups. One effect of this was the common division of islands or island territories into senior and junior halves, or moieties, throughout Polynesia. On Niue, the head or face of the land was the senior half, and the junior land was also called *uluhiku,* meaning "tail of the fish." In New Zealand, very similarly, the two main islands were conceived as fish lying head to head, with the head of Maui's fish (Te Upoko ō te Ika ā Maui) at Cook Strait and the tail of Maui's fish (Te Hiku o te Ika ā Maui, or *muriwhenua,* the back lands) in the far north. Likewise, the southern tail of the South Island fish was called *murihiku.* A drawing in 1793 by Tuki, a northern Māori chief, depicts the North Island as divided longitudinally by a common pathway, Te Ara Tapu, along which the spirits of the dead could proceed unhindered to the northwestern headland, there to enter the underworld by slipping into the sea. It is possible, although there is no specific evidence, that the pathway also separated eastern and western lands into senior and junior sides.

Island moieties were subdivided by seniority. It is not so clear how this worked in New Zealand, although it is not difficult to see that in Ngāi Tahu tribal lands in the South Island, for example, the older or more powerful clans, being those closest in lineage to the tribes' founders, took the most productive lands. Consistent with the low level of political integration in New Zealand, Māori rights in land and other resources were exclusive rights at the level at which they were held, by an individual, *whānau* (family), *hapū* (clan), or *iwi* (tribe). Several *whānau* might hold bundles of rights in the same gardening lands, but the rights could not be to the same places within those lands. *Hapū* (clans or subtribes) and *whānau* claimed exclusive rights in hunting grounds and fisheries—*wahi mahinga kai* (places for getting food)—and set out parcels of land or other resources for the exclusive use of each group. *Iwi* claimed exclusive rights in their common land. Disputes were often intractable, but they were not resolved by agreeing to share the same assets. They had to be taken by one party or divided, amicably or otherwise. Modern beliefs about Māori groups having indistinct boundaries, sharing property rights, or holding overlapping rights in the sense of sharing them are inimical to traditional concepts. Chief Justice Sir William Martin wrote in 1846 (quoted by N. Smith in 1942) that "there might be several conflicting claimants of the same land; but however the natives might be divided amongst themselves as to the validity of any of the several claims, still no man doubted that there was in every case a right of property subsisting in some one of the claimants."

Māori, and Chatham Islands Moriori, exhibited a "traditional" type of Polynesian society in which continuous status differentiation presented fewer opportunities to exercise power than in open or stratified East Polynesian societies. Group membership in South Polynesia was fluid through weakly restricted rules of descent by ancestry, and effective authority was limited to the level of the clan. Limited societal stratification and a low level of political integration confined most religious activity to familial levels, and large, stone-built religious structures equivalent to *heiau, marae,* and *ahu* (loosely, temples) in East Polynesia were absent. Demographic trends and changing climatic conditions were especially significant in shaping the social and political structures of the Māori population.

WORKING THE LAND

At the time of initial colonization, the absolute and relative abundance of land in New Zealand was phenomenal, with about 1,000 square kilometers per individual (0.001 people per square kilometer), and even after 150 years, when the total population might have reached 5,000–8,000, it would still have been only 0.02–0.03 people per square kilometer. Yet, despite such extremely low density during the early years of Māori settlement, substantial changes were wrought in the resource landscape. The first and most visible was the loss of forest by burning, a process accelerated by the inherent vulnerability of New Zealand trees to fire and their slow rates of recovery. Before human arrival nearly 90 percent of the land was covered in forest or shrubland, but within 150 years of initial colonization 40 percent of the South Island forest was gone and about 15 percent of the North Island forest.

Rates of deforestation reflected a broad environmental division in New Zealand between a windward province of humid climates and dense forest and a leeward province of dry climates and open forest, which was also reflected in subsistence histories. The nine species of *moa* (flightless birds), ranging in mean bodyweight from 25 to 140 kilograms, occurred mainly in the leeward province, as is evident from numerous processing sites (figure 6.2), some of which extended over 50 hectares and contained the remains of tens of thousands of birds. Although *moa* population densities were around four birds per square kilometer, according to calculations in 2019 by A. D. M. Latham and others in *Ecography,* and the total population of all species prior to hunting was possibly two million, this slow-breeding megafaunal family was driven into extinction by the mid-fifteenth century at relatively modest rates of human predation. Another megafaunal resource was the New Zealand fur

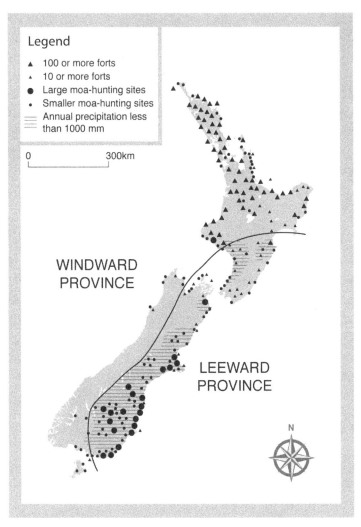

Figure 6.2. Map of the windward and leeward environmental provinces of New Zealand showing the distribution of low precipitation, moa hunting sites (early in the sequence), and *pā*, or forts (late in the sequence).

seal. A population of about three million inhabited the New Zealand coast before human arrival, especially around the southern South Island. Breeding rookeries were vulnerable to sustained Māori predation, and the fur seal population had declined to one million by the eighteenth century. The rapid loss or decline of the large faunal taxa still left abundant faunal resources of marine fish and shellfish, freshwater fish (notably eels), ground-nesting seabirds, ducks, quail, rails, tree-nesting pigeons, parrots, and many other species. Native plant foods were scarce, but bracken fern root and the roots and stems of native *ti* provided starch and sugar.

An alternative food source that the progenitors of Māori depended upon was agriculture. Of the few cultigens that survived in New Zealand, *uhi* (yam) and *ti* were largely confined to the northern North Island, *taro* and bottle gourd reached the southern North Island and possibly the northwestern tip of the South Island, and *kumara* (sweet potato) could be grown down to the Kaikoura district on the east coast of the South Island and possibly as far south as Banks Peninsula. The common assumption that all the cultigens arrived in the migration period now seems incorrect, especially in regard to *kumara,* which was by far the most important crop and which might not have been available until the fifteenth century. From then on, however, there was substantial *kumara* gardening in the North Island—that is, from Taranaki and Hawkes Bay to the north, as marked by the distribution of *pā* (fortified) sites, which are closely linked to cultivation (see figure 6.2).

Horticulture in the northern North Island took advantage of soils formed in areas of recent volcanic activity. Tephritic soils (formed from tephra, volcanic material that is deposited from the air) occur over about 40 percent of the North Island, but pumice soils (formed from large particles with very low density), which occur mainly in the northeast, represent almost half of this total. Pumice soils are formed from very young, weakly consolidated sediments that are low in clay content and deficient in major nutrients and trace elements. However, allophanic soils, which represent nearly one-third of all tephritic soils on the North Island and are found mainly toward the west, are formed on fine-grained layers of tephra. These soils are deep and mostly 10,000 to 25,000 years old. They are named for their dominant clay mineral, allophane, which occurs as nanocrystalline particles with a relatively huge surface area, which facilitates a high capacity for water storage and for soil nutrient exchange with plants. Allophanic soils have high organic carbon content and good aeration and water retention, and they are free draining, even after heavy rain. Easy to dig and weed, they are distributed mainly across smooth, tephra-mantled landscapes in the inland Bay of Islands, South Auckland, inland Waikato, the western Bay of Plenty, and Taranaki. Substantial garden areas (550 hectares) have been recorded around the Pouerua *pā* in the inland Bay of Islands, and there are about 2,000 hectares of gardens around the volcanic cones on the Tamaki Isthmus, Auckland. The most extensive garden area is in the middle Waikato basin, where about 3,000–4,000 hectares of soils have been modified by Māori cultivation.

In that district, gardens were built by the burning and felling of primary forest, after which the existing soil was modified by the addition of sands and gravels dug from beneath it in the borrow pits located near the gardens. This was a laborious procedure. To modify one hectare of soil required the digging, transport, and spreading of 1,300 cubic meters of sand and gravel; 4,000 hectares would have required five million cubic meters to be dug up and distributed. Of course, only a proportion of the gardens were in use at once, partly because they seem to have been built over a period extending from the sixteenth to the eighteenth centuries and also because they were swiddens, or shifting cultivations—that is, gardens used for several years until the soil fertility declined, then abandoned to regrowing forest for perhaps 7–20 years to recover.

Modern experimental plots of *kumara* cultivation have averaged 12 tonnes of *kumara* per hectare, which would provide almost 3,500 person-days of an exclusively *kumara* diet, or 4.6 months of food for 25 people. If, in a swiddening system, 600 hectares of the central Waikato gardens were in use at any one time, they could have produced enough food for 15,000 people for the winter, May to September. Clearly, large-scale *kumara* production could have made a substantial difference in population-carrying capacity in northern New Zealand. If that was the case by the fifteenth century, then it could be expected that intensive food production would have been accompanied by vigorous and sustained population growth.

Growing People

The total size of the Māori population in 1800 was 100,000 to 200,000. There is uncertainty about this, just as there is about estimates of total population at the time of European contact in most Polynesian islands. Recent estimates are generally much higher than they were, and the upper figure for New Zealand is not implausible. Even so, differences in population density between South and East Polynesia were large, around two orders of magnitude, too large to be explained by historical mistakes in estimating population sizes or by errors in retrodictive techniques. By 1800, Māori population density was 0.4–0.8 people per square kilometer, compared to about 16 per square kilometer in Hawai'i and 35 per square kilometer in the Cook Islands. There were 11 people per square kilometer of arable land in New Zealand, which is low by tropical East Polynesian standards of 100 to 120 people per square kilometer of arable land. Considering the much greater area of arable land available in New Zealand, why were population size and density not greater?

There may be several reasons. One is simply that because of the later age of colonization in South Polynesia, 200 years or more later than in central East Polynesia, there was less time for population growth. Another is that high population densities in tropical Polynesia were facilitated by low seasonality, year-round root and tree crop growth in high temperatures across a broad altitudinal range, and a wide diversity of crops. In New Zealand, by contrast, gardening depended very largely upon one cultigen, *kumara* (sweet potato), grown as a single seasonal crop, with yields stored to provide food to people during the winter (nongrowing) season. A consequence of limited agricultural capacity was inhibition of population growth and so of societal complexity in New Zealand.

In tropical Polynesia, with political organization of labor, population densities (people per square kilometer) reached 15–20 in the Hawaiian Islands, 45 in Tonga, and 70 in Tahiti, often with human population densities exceeding 200 people per square kilometer in particularly productive districts. The circumstances of South Polynesia maintained a dispersed, clan-based population in which few polities attained the consumer density sufficient to require intensive food production, or could command the necessary labor, until late in the pre-European era, and then only in some northern districts. In those, population density (assuming a total population of 100,000) reached about 1 person per square kilometer, but it was 0.25 people per square kilometer in central New Zealand, where agriculture was marginal, and only 0.02 people per square kilometer in the southern region, where agriculture was absent. The regional differences in population density reflect, in part though not wholly, the demographic boost of cultivating *kumara* in an environment where natural sources of edible starch were relatively scarce, and those natural sources of starch that did exist were more common in the north than elsewhere. In other words, without horticulture, the Māori population density overall in 1800 would probably have remained somewhere between the central and southern densities.

The regional distribution of population density was the culmination of growth rates across the previous 500 years. Using the summed probability distribution of radiocarbon dates in 2019, A. A. Brown and E. R. Crema showed, in the *Journal of Island and Coastal Archaeology,* that Māori population growth generally followed a logistic growth curve, but with regional variations. The overall pattern was one of rapid growth up to about 1500–1550 and then leveling off up to the nineteenth century. In the southern region (the South Island except for the north and northeast coast) population growth was very strong up to about 1400, at which point it dropped rapidly and remained negative up to the eighteenth century. This looks very much like a boom and bust situation. In the central area (northern South Island and southern North Island) there was moderate population growth in a stepped pattern, with growth steps about 1400 and 1650, the latter of which continued up to about 1800. The early step might reflect migration of southern Māori into the central region. In the northern region (northern half of the North Island) growth rates were lower than expected up to about 1450 and then began to surge strongly up to the seventeenth century.

The northern pattern is consistent with other observations. As R. Newnham and others argued in 2018, in *The Holocene,* deforestation in the northern region was relatively minor shortly after human colonization but took off in the fifteenth century. *Pā* construction also began in the late fifteenth century and appears to have accelerated from the sixteenth to the eighteenth century. These two indicators, together with the population growth curve, indicate a relatively late development of large-scale horticulture.

An additional consideration in patterns and rates of Māori demography is climate change. There were, of course, fluctuations in tropical climates at centenary scales across the Pacific, notably by variations in the frequency of ENSO—fluctuations in ocean surface temperature and atmospheric pressure—and movement of the Intertropical Convergence Zone, but in South Polynesia, where introduced horticulture reached its margins, relatively small changes in temperature and rainfall could induce substantial responses in the range of crops or in their yields.

CLIMATE CHANGE AND SETTLEMENT PATTERN RESPONSES

During the Polynesian Warm Period (which corresponds to the global Medieval Warm Period), about 1000–1380 CE, New Zealand had warm and humid conditions everywhere. There was then an abrupt switch, in about 1400, to wet, cloudy, and cold conditions that prevailed everywhere until the mid-sixteenth century; thereafter conditions remained wet in southern New Zealand but became cool and dry in the north up to the early eighteenth century. Correspondingly, the Global Little Ice Age spans 1385–1710, and it was most severely wet, cold, and windy in the period 1500–1650.

In southern New Zealand, the flush of *moa*-hunting, which had probably supported several thousand people, represented by at least 255 *moa*-hunting sites south of Banks Peninsula, was drawing to a close at the end of the Polynesian Warm Period and brought *moa* to extinction by 1450; there was a parallel decline of sealing. Of radiocarbon-dated sites within a radius of 200 kilometers from Shag River Mouth, north Otago, 36 date to earlier than 1450, but only 10 to 1450–1650. No large coastal settlements remained; occupation on the south coast had effectively ceased, and much of the interior was abandoned. Whether there was outward migration, to the northern South Island for example, is unknown archaeologically or in the traditions, but it might have formed part of the stepped pattern in population growth in the central region.

In central New Zealand, gardens on both coasts of the southern North Island were not occupied later than the fifteenth or early sixteenth centuries. Similar sites date to the fifteenth and sixteenth centuries in the Marlborough Sounds, Tasman Bay, and Golden Bay, although some persisted until the end of the seventeenth century in Golden Bay. These data suggest that by the late sixteenth century *kumara* (sweet potato) cultivation no longer existed south of about latitude 41° south, representing a retreat northward of around 150 kilometers from Kaikoura and implying a decline in mean annual temperature at sea level of about 1°C. Furthermore, just as gardening was relatively scarce between its absolute southern limit and Tasman Bay, so it is probable that by the sixteenth century gardening north of the new southern limit was marginal up to southern Hawkes Bay and South Taranaki.

Climate change seems a plausible explanation for the retreat of gardening, if not necessarily the only one. *Kumara* will not yield in soil temperatures of less than 15°C for five consecutive months, conditions barely met in central New Zealand even today. Tree-ring records, to take a typical one from the western South Island, show a drop in mean summer temperature of 1.0 to 1.5°C between 1480 and 1525, and an oxygen-isotope record from Hawkes Bay shows the same sharp dip in temperature in 1500 and a deterioration into climate conditions described, in 2008, as very wet and very cold by Andrew Lorrey and colleagues in *Quaternary International*. A summer temperature decline of 0.8 to 1.4°C, relative to today, might not seem like much, but that scale of change is very similar to data for the Little Ice Age in Europe, where profound economic and social consequences have been recorded.

In the northern North Island *kumara* cultivation remained viable, although rapid development in gardening in the inland Waikato might reflect movement into a drier climate as well as the exploitation of the allophanic soils. The main change, however, was the consolidation of population growth in the northern North Island, probably as the result of gardening suppression or loss farther south as the Little Ice Age intensified. Whether or not *kumara* arrived later than the other cultigens, development of its extensive cultivation seems to have been delayed until the sixteenth to eighteenth centuries, when Little Ice Age conditions turned drier in the north.

WARFARE AND MIGRATION

The visibility of Māori archaeology becomes greatly enhanced from the late fifteenth century by the construction of *pā* sites, especially in the northern North Island (see figure 6.2), and this phenomenon is paralleled chronologically by a fairly abrupt switch in the focus of Māori tradition toward warfare and internal migration. Numerous oral narratives, in most cases interstitial to extensive *whakapapa* (genealogies), were recorded by early European observers. Māori, unlike Hawaiians and Tahitians, retained the political independence of *iwi* (tribes) and *hapū* (clans or subtribes) up into the European era, and each polity, of which there were hundreds, had its own *whakapapa* and traditions stretching back to the founding canoes. There are detailed accounts of the motives and movements of warfare within and across tribal boundaries and of migrations that preceded or followed the acquisition of new lands.

This is readily understood in terms of oral traditions, whose primary function beyond a record of lineages was to link individuals and groups to their possessions, current or claimed. Consequently, periods of settlement mobility and social ferment, when land and other assets were often redistributed and political relationships realigned, needed to be fixed in the group memory with clarity and precision. The later traditional history describes frequent fighting and extensive volatility in territorial control, especially in the 10–12 generations before the arrival of Europeans. The causes of trouble were given as grievances held by chiefs, most over insults involving food or women, but those proximate issues concealed deeper problems arising, it can be inferred, from political divisions and resource competition that emerged with population growth.

From the early sixteenth century on, these divisions were also manifested by group migrations, generally hostile, mostly from north to south and especially in eastern districts. Ngāti Awa who were living in northern Northland, coming under pressure from Ngāti Whatua and Ngāpuhi, migrated south, about the middle of the seventeenth century, to the Auckland Isthmus and then to Taranaki, where they became known as Te Ati Awa, and then on to join their ancestral relatives in the Bay of Plenty. In the early eighteenth century, Ngā Puhi expanded east and south in Northland, all the way down to the Kaipara Harbour, and Tuhoe expanded their territory southeast and west and eventually reached north to the Bay of Plenty. Similar movements were occurring elsewhere.

There was also a series of migrations southward in the North Island and across to the South Island, in each case involving major *hapū* but by no means all of each *iwi* concerned. Migration of broadly related clans from the East Coast, North Island, began around the beginning of the sixteenth century with Ngāti Mamoe moving to the South Island East Coast and Ngāti Wairaki and Ngāti Tumatakokiri to the western South Island. Ngāti Kahungunu, Ngāti Ira, and Ngāi

Tahu moved to Wellington in the sixteenth century, and then Ngāi Tahu moved into the South Island by a series of migrations that continued into the eighteenth century. The migrations were initially overland to reach Cook Strait but then more often by canoe down the coast of the South Island. The seafaring involved a new type of canoe, the war canoe, a large single-hulled vessel, up to 35 meters long, which was generally paddled, though sometimes a small double spritsail was hoisted when the canoe was traveling downwind. The advantages of the war canoe over sailing canoes for expeditions intent upon capturing new territories were that it could carry 100 warriors or more, sufficient to overwhelm most settlements, and that it was fast over a short distance, facilitating attacks before coastal communities had time to organize their defenses.

One feature typical of the late traditional migrations is worth emphasizing. The direction of migration was almost exclusively from north to south, which is generally away from districts of higher population density and greater agricultural activity, as is evident from the distribution of *pā* sites. About 7,000 *pā* have been recorded, and 98 percent are in the North Island, most of them in the northern district. *Pā* had clear defensive functions, to protect gardens, people, and stored garden produce, but they were also prominently visible statements of group strength and centers of ritual and religious activity, as discussed by Atholl Anderson in *Monuments and People in the Pacific*. In the southern North Island *pā* density drops noticeably, and *pā* are relatively scarce in the South Island. The clan migrations, then, were clearly out of the preferred horticultural districts and into areas marginal for gardening or beyond (figure 6.3).

At one level, as described at length in the tribal traditions, the migrations are readily explained by cycles of interclan disputes; the only practical recourse in many cases was for one

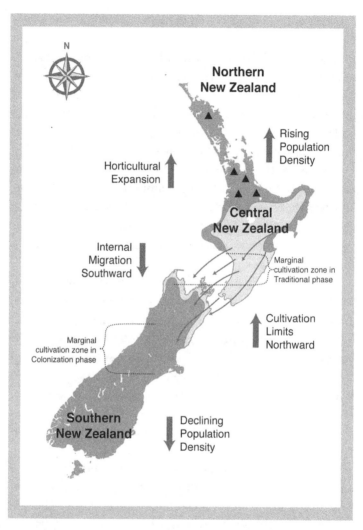

Figure 6.3. Map of northern, central (light shading), and southern New Zealand showing the changes that occurred during the middle centuries of the New Zealand sequence, 1400–1600. Population density declined in the south, and it rose in the north with horticultural expansion and *pā* building. In the central region, the zone of marginal cultivation moved north, and there was substantial southward migration.

group to move away, and that often meant moving south into an area with fewer people and more natural resources. At a deeper level, several potential incentives to migrate south can be identified. As population increased toward the north, and both economic and military power developed an asymmetry that increasingly favored the north, the vast and sparsely inhabited South Island, with its rich natural resources, including all the sources of jade, the major prestige item, must have become proportionately more desirable. Increasing marginalization of horticulture around Hawkes Bay during the Little Ice Age could have triggered competition for garden land, pushing some groups into migration. It is also possible that an increasing scale of horticulture in the northern North Island generated a demand for labor that led to slave raiding in the marginal areas of the central North Island, thereby giving an incentive for some people in those areas to move away. In the early nineteenth century, when cultivation of the newly introduced white potato was expanding rapidly in Northland to fuel trade with Europeans, especially for muskets, it was certainly a practice of northern tribes to raid the eastern tribes in Coromandel, in the Bay of Plenty, and down the East Coast for slave labor. The cluster of demographic, subsistence, and settlement pattern changes during the middle centuries of Māori tenure are shown in figure 6.3.

Land and People

I have focused here on mainland New Zealand, but the outlying islands are also interesting in several respects. In most of them, settlement ceased fairly soon after discovery, and they had long been uninhabited by the time of European arrival. Raoul Island in the Kermadecs is an active volcano, and the archaeological sites there are covered in layers of ash, pumice, and volcanic mud, the possible cause of abandoned occupation. At least some of the people sailed 1,300 kilometers west to Norfolk Island, where they established a settlement that survived for perhaps 200 years. Subsistence was strongly focused on the exploitation of nesting procellarids, and the site might have been abandoned when those populations were driven close to extinction, as almost happened in the early days of European settlement. The Norfolk Polynesians, uniquely in South Polynesia so far as is known, constructed a ritual site of stone slabs and uprights, with a buried elephant seal skull and with obsidian flaked liberally over the platform. Some people from Norfolk Island likely fetched up on the east coast of Australia, where an early East Polynesian adze of Norfolk Island basalt ended up in a midden. The east to west movement, rather than movement back to New Zealand, might reflect the difficulty of sailing against the southeast trade winds.

The only continuous occupation was in the Chatham Islands, a cool, cloudy archipelago located in the subtropical convergence zone east of New Zealand. Moriori, like southern Māori from whom they probably descended, were complex foragers, exploiting cast-up whales—a common bounty there—seals, albatrosses, and other marine birds, and fish and shellfish. They also caught eels, dug fern root, and tended and harvested groves of kopi (*Corynocarpus laevigatus; karaka* in New Zealand), which provided abundant berries that were processed for carbohydrates. The Moriori population, perhaps reaching 3,000 in total, is distinctive in Polynesia for its renunciation, beyond first blood, of warfare among the clans. In the early nineteenth century, however, Māori invaded the Chathams and killed, enslaved, or otherwise subjugated the Moriori.

The land-people relationships of Māori in New Zealand were remarkable for their regional variety, sharpened as they were by the impact of the Little Ice Age, which created cold, windy, and wet conditions that closed down agriculture in central New Zealand, especially in the middle centuries of Māori tenure. Once the early resource boom in *moas* and seals was over, by about 1450 in the southern region, most of the southern South Island was either abandoned or lightly occupied, even perhaps occupied only during seasonal forays in the warmer months. Once the *hapū* (clan or subtribe) migrations began, late in the sequence, most of the South Island became a region of complex foraging. Large villages were fully occupied during the winter but largely vacated at other times of the year as families pursued their seasonal rounds of marine fishing, eeling, muttonbirding, forest fowling, fern root and *ti* processing, and the gathering of a wide range of industrial and domestic resources.

Landholding was mainly at the *hapū* level, but settlements were often composed of family groups with different *hapū* affiliations. This had the advantage that most *hapū* would then have a stake in local resources throughout the *iwi* (tribal) territory. That was especially important for pan-tribal access to the rich seasonal harvest of muttonbirds, or sooty shearwaters, which, preserved in their own fat in airtight kelp bags, were traded throughout the South Island and into the lower North Island. Indeed, the success of Ngāi Tahu economy and society was based very considerably upon food preservation and exchange networks within the *iwi* and beyond.

Cabbage tree (*Cordyline australis*) sugar and bracken fern rhizomes, dried marine fish and eels, and preserved rails and forest birds were other prominent sources of subsistence and exchange. Seafaring, mostly using the double canoe, enabled people to journey up to 1,800 kilometers back and forth to exploit seasonal resources, while bundle boats made from dried flax-flower stalks were used on lakes and rivers. Trade to the North Island also included luxury items, especially weapons and ornaments, made from South Island jade, sometimes in return for dried *kumara*. Trade to the North Island was facilitated by the historical circumstance that Ngāi Tahu had arrived fairly recently in the South Island and still retained social connections in the North Island. Although Ngāi Tahu held a territory the size of Wisconsin, with a dispersed settlement pattern and a relatively small population (perhaps 3,000–5,000 people at most), they managed to maintain a tribal chiefdom with a hierarchy of regional and local chiefs. To a significant extent, the foraging and subsistence exchange model of southern New Zealand was fundamental to Māori society everywhere, although its subsistence significance declined toward the north with the availability of horticulture. Throughout Māori society, descent remained the foundation of identity, but in the relatively populous and horticulturally sustained north, political evolution seems to have begun by the seventeenth century. In the course of the increasing warfare and predatory migrations described in the later Māori traditions, the traditions themselves were being revised to reinforce the political standing of powerful lineages by emphasizing particular links to some important ancestors rather than others, as among the Ngā Puhi *iwi* in Northland and among the Waikato people. This can be construed as the first step toward a more centralized form of Indigenous governance, as in Tahiti or Hawai'i, which might have developed further under conditions of continued population growth and territorial stress, had the arrival of Europeans been delayed some centuries longer.

III

Comparisons and Syntheses

7

The Hidden *Pā* of Knowledge
and the Mind of Māori

Te Maire Tau

One of New Zealand's great scholars, Anne Salmond, provided a superb reference in an early article of the 1980s when she recalled the great New Zealand scholar of the turn of the nineteenth century, Elsdon Best. After many years of research, Best confessed that he had seen only "the outer palisades of the hidden pa of knowledge." This is an utterly intriguing statement, because any scholar of Māori knows very well how rich, dense, and full Best's research, publications, and engagement with Māori had been. The vertical depth of Best's archives that cover the creation traditions down to the migration traditions of *iwi* (tribes), *hapū* (clans or subtribes), and *whānau* (families) is both rich and complex enough to delight not only historians but also experts in our language and traditions. Likewise, the horizontal breadth of his material, from genealogies of tribes, to the chants that celebrate the births, deaths, and actions of chiefs, to the actual food-gathering traditions of *iwi*, *hapū*, and *whānau* is at times remarkable. So, too, are the beauty of the tone poems, the sayings special to each tribe, and his observations of elders of his time. Yet Elsdon Best still understood that he remained beyond the outer palisades when it came to the "hidden pa of knowledge."

What Best meant when he referred to the hidden pa of knowledge is, to me, an intriguing question. For non–New Zealand readers, a *pā* is a fortified village common among Māori in the nineteenth century. Today, the term *pā* is used to describe villages and reserves where Māori now live. In traditional fortifications, the *pā* was defended by a series of palisades and trenches. Best knew as well as anyone else what the inside of a *pā* looked like. He was also aware that he knew more than most about the traditional knowledge taught inside the *whare wānanga*, or *whare pūrākau* —the traditional buildings where sacred knowledge was passed on from tribal elders to the next generation. In short, few Western scholars other than Best had access to the hidden knowledge he sought. Yet, here Best was, still outside, looking into the *pā*.

What was this hidden knowledge that Best sought? My guess is that Best was not talking about knowledge as much as he was talking about the "mind" of Māori. Best knew that Māori located and understood the mind to be something vastly different from what nineteenth-century European thought considered it. He was also aware that the ways in which Māori saw and understood the world and the ways in which the internal Māori mind configured that world were also vastly different from Western ways and configurations. Māori configured time, space, and the environment differently, and these sectors had a synchronic relationship with the culture of Māori. At the center of time, space, environment, and culture was the mind. It was the mind that Best struggled to understand, because for Māori the mind was quite different from what Best understood the mind to be.

So when we confront the question of our Māori relationship to the environment and then our very identity, my initial
reaction is to wade into this swamp of debate and to engage
with current theories and propositions already placed in the
mix by a wide range of scholars. But this is where we need to
pause and recalibrate. Even that word "swamp" denotes something different to Māori and outside minds. For Māori, the
pu-kanohi, the lagoons along the estuaries, are rich areas of
food, life, and identity. Many in the West would see these sites
differently; indeed, when European settlers arrived, they very
quickly set about draining our food places to reclaim new land
from the lagoon beds and wetlands.

I accept the point made in previous chapters that Polynesians lived differently on the various islands that they discovered,
and differently within parts of complex islands and archipelagoes, and even (as is illustrated by the consequences of a changing climate in Aotearoa) that they lived differently at the same
place at various times in their history. The questions that I will
consider here are "What is the mind of Māori, and what do
Māori see when they look at the natural world?" These two
basic questions are the building blocks of *mātauranga Māori,*
which is now a term in Aotearoa, on Te Wai Pounamu (the
South Island), for "Māori knowledge" systems or, better still,
an epistemology that is Māori. I focus on Māori in part because
my knowledge and experience are here, but also because in
many ways New Zealand in general, and Te Wai Pounamu in
particular, is an outlier among Pacific islands environmentally
and, consequently, in the ways Māori lived. If, as I will suggest,
Māori minds are like those of their relatives on other Pacific
islands, then the ways people lived may have changed with
conditions on different islands, but how they perceived the
world did not change. The starting position for this chapter is
this notion: "the world is not what we think it is; it's what we

think it is." To explain this, I am going to start with the first proposition: that our people thought the world into being.

In 1849, one of our most learned priests, Matiaha Tiramōrehu, decided to record the creation tradition of his tribe, Ngāi Tahu. Matiaha, or Mathias, his biblical name, opened his narrative with a phrase that is common among tribal creation chants, "*Kei a te po, te timatanga mai o te waiatatanga mai a te atua*" (quoted in M. Van Bellekom and R. Harlow, *Te Waiatatanga mai o te Atua*). Nearly every scholar has translated the passage this way: "In the night we start with the creation chant of the gods." The translation is simple and direct. It is also wrong, because it assumes that Matiaha is reciting a lineal tradition of creation like those we find in most cultures. It is more likely that Matiaha was invoking the gods, or *atua*, into being through his chant.

Twenty years earlier, when Matiaha was learning the traditions, he did so at the great fortified village of Kaiapoi in the South Island. Only the designated sons of senior chiefs were allowed to enter the sacred schools of learning, the *whare pūrākau*. The building that these sons were being taught in was supported by giant carved pillars along the walls, all of which were ancestral figures. Before either the high priests or the students entered the building these carved figures would have been smothered with the blood of a slave killed in the morning. More than likely, a variation of the following words would have been chanted to the ancestors and *atua* as they entered the building (my translation):

Ka tirohia mai koutou i	You observe from above,
Runga nga whatu kura o te rangi	my heavenly ancestors,
Ka hotu tonu ake te ngakau	the heart that still beats onward

Ki te hotu o te ihirangi	to the breaking of the dawn.
Ka kitea koutou nga taonga	You see the treasures
E tu nei,	that stand here,
E te iwi,	Oh my people,
E te mana	those with authority and noble descent,
E te tapu	those who are sacred,
Te wehi	those who cast a shadow of power,
Te ihi	those who cast a shadow of life.
Te urutapu i houa ki te atua	The sacred vessels dedicated to the gods
I huru pikitia ai tenei ohora!	whose hair has been bound, awake!
Kua tata nei ki te whakakapinga	and draw near as this ritual ends
Mo koutou nga taonga	for the treasures dedicated to you.

When these rituals were undertaken, the carved posts were seen as living beings. Outside on the porch of the building was an elderly woman, who sat there through the night. This elder was a *ruahine,* also known as the *pa-whaka-wairua.* The task of the elderly woman was to hold the *mauri,* or sacred essence, of the school during its sessions. We know that when our elders gathered to teach their students sacred knowledge, they did so at night, which is captured in the first phrase they chanted when reciting the origins of their world, "*Kei a te po*" (In the night). For Māori, our dead lived with Hine-nui-te-po, the "Great Mother of the Night." Night is when the teaching commenced, and Hine-nui-te-po and the night were one and the same.

Therefore the dead were being invoked, making the context one of high sacredness and one where the ancestors were being called to return.

With the context set I would suggest the following interpretation of Matiaha's manuscript: "In the night, we commence with chanting the gods into being."

In the first translation we simply see Matiaha Tiramōrehu and other tribal high priests gathered in their colleges of learning, teaching their students the creation traditions by chanting them. In the second translation, Matiaha does more than recite—he invites the gods into his world. And who are the gods that he invokes in an isolated South Island fishing village in the winter of 1849? Matiaha invokes the *hau,* the winds, and in particular, on this night, the southerly wind that brings Te Kohu, the mist, and the damage that occurs with the *atua* who is the southerly wind, Te Wawahiwhare, "the Battering of Houses." These are more than likely the *atua* that spoke to Matiaha Tiramōrehu on June 9, 1849.

For Māori, this is why ancestral manuscripts that hold the genealogies of the ancestors and *atua* are so important. The manuscripts hold the *mauri* (essence) of their ancestors, who are invoked when the books are opened and chanted. The idea of chanting one's ancestors and gods into being is known to all Māori.

The North Island scholar Te Rangikaheke dictated an account to Te Whiwhi in 1851 recording an episode in history in which the chief Manaia sought his brother-in-law, Ngātoro-i-rangi, to avenge an earlier fight. Manaia and Ngātoro-i-rangi met and agreed to fight the following morning. Ngātoro-i-rangi was vulnerable because his people were absent, but Manaia and his fleet were settled below his fort. With the agreement made, Ngātoro-i-rangi set about invoking the gods, by *karakia,* by chanting them into the world:

Ka noho Ngātoro i tana pā. Ka ahiahi, ka noho
Ngātoro ki te tūāhu karakia ai. I te pō ka tomo ki
roto i tō rāua whare ko te ruahine. Ko te mahi tonu
tūrā he karakia, e kumekume ana i ngā hau o te
rangi. Ko te ope e mahi ana tūrā i te tākaro, i te
haka, i te waiata, i te ngahau. Tā te ope whaihanga,
he ngahau, kāore e mōhio ka mate rātou. Ki tā rātou
nei mahara, ko Ngātoro e mate, ko te kotahi.

The scholar Jane McRae (in her 2017 book *Maori Oral Tradition*)
translates the passage as follows:

Ngātoro remained in his fort. When it was evening,
Ngātoro sat at the altar to pray. At night he and his
wife [the use of 'ruahine' is suggestive of her role as
older woman in the prayer ritual] went into their
house. His constant occupation there was prayer,
drawing in the winds of heaven. As for the [invad-
ing] party, they were engaged in games, dances
with chants, songs, entertainment. The party, pre-
occupied with entertainment, were not aware that
they would die. To their mind it was Ngātoro who
would die, just the one.

What I have tried to show so far is that when our elders
invoked the *atua,* they invoked the wind, because the wind was
seen as the *atua.* For Māori, the wind is the *hau* and breath (*hā*)
of the gods and their presence. In our creation traditions, the
winds are descendants of Raki and his first wife. Raki, or
Rangi, as most New Zealanders know, is the sky. What is not
widely known is that his first wife was Poko-harua-te-po. Poko-
harua-te-po was seen as the source of *hau*, which is best understood as the wind or the breath of life. Our Ngāi Tahu tribal

priest Waruwarutu said of this *atua*, "*Ko ngāuri, he hau katoa, ko ngākarakia, ngātapu*" (The descendants were all the winds and the incantations and *tapu*). What is important here is that we avoid heading down a rabbit hole and interpreting these words as separate ideas, because the point being made is that in the beginning are the gods (*atua*) and their physical manifestation is the wind, which is in turn their breath. For Māori, life starts with breath. These were the *atua* Matiaha invoked at the start of this chapter.

Once the breath of the *atua* was established, the ancestors followed, or, more properly, the land followed. The best way to describe what our ancestors saw when they looked at the landscape is that they saw a physical representation of their ancestors. In the genealogy that follows the high priests, Wi Pokuku again invokes the gods, tracing his descent from Rākaihautū, the first ancestor to land in the South Island. Wi Pokuku then traces descent from Rākaihautū down to himself. As a bare recital, outsiders would simply see a chronology of ancestors, but what our people saw was a statement of being with the land. This is what is meant by the "hidden *pa* of knowledge." To make this easier to understand, I have managed to identify most of the ancestors to the landscape and, in particular, to the Hawea-Wanaka region in the hinterland of the South Island. Rākaihautū and Te Rokohouia are father and son, respectively, and the names from Te Awe-ariki down to Te Whatu-karokata are ancestors and references to the Southern Alps, which dominate this island.

Rākaihautū	–	
Rokohouia	=	
Te Awe-ariki	=	
Te Aweawe	=	
Te Whatu	=	(Peak on the Southern Alps)

Te Whatu-hunahuna	=	(Peak on the Southern Alps)
Te Whatu-karokaro	=	(Peak on the Southern Alps)
Te Whatu-ariki	=	(Peak on the Southern Alps)
Te Whatu-karokata	=	(Peak on the Southern Alps)
Tāne-auroa	=	(Crown Range)
Tititea	=	(Mount Aspriing)
Te Waitakaia	=	(Hill at the south end of Lake Wanaka)
Autaia	=	(An island in the Maranuku River)
Taki-porotu	=	(Tributary leading into the Ahuriri River)
Hautumua	=	
Turaki-potiki	=	(Mountain peak on the southwest side of Lake Hawea)
Aupawha	=	(Tributary that flows into Hawea from the southwest)
Huripopoiarua	=	(Tributary that flows into Lake Hawea on the northwest side)
Pekerakitahi	=	(Mount Kinross, Manuhaaia Flat, Lake Hawea)
Waikorire	=	(Wai-rere Falls)
Ruatea	=	(Mount Doris)
Para-karehu	=	(Eastern side of Lake Wanaka on the peninsula before Te Waikakahi)
Roko-te-whatu	=	(Range just above the Neck, or Lake Hawea)
Te Rahere	=	(Tributary that runs into Wanaka, north-eastern side)
Tuawhiti	=	(Creek that flows into Lake Wanaka from the northeast side)
Upoko-hapa	=	
Kura-whaiana	=	
Pokeka-wera	=	(Five *mahinga kai* sites down from Tiori Patea)
Turihuka	=	(Silver Island, Dingleburn Lagoon)
Te Paetara (Paetarariki)	=	(Island at the south end of Lake Hawea)

Taku	=	(*Pā* site at the northern entrance to Lake Ohau)
Te Waimatau	=	(Lagoon near Lake Ohau on the western side)
Upoko-ruru	=	(Flat on the southern end of Lake Ohau)
Te Whatukaao	=	Maramarua (Young River, which runs into Makarora River)
Punahikoia	=	Te Rakitamau (Mount Cuthbert, Waitaki Valley)
Hikitia-teraki	=	Kopiri
Taka-o-Te Raki	=	Kohana
Pitorua	=	Iwi-paoa
Te Waipunahau	=	Tupai
Te Keteke-wahi	=	Te Aohikuraki
Puawhe	=	Haeata
Mata Teka	=	Kauae
Wi Pokuku	=	

There are a number of variations to this genealogy, depending on the landmarks. However, what the genealogies indicate is a relationship that connects Pokuku to the landscape, the rivers, mountains, and waterways and ultimately to his ancestors. The critical point to understand here is that in this worldview, Pokuku's ancestors were not located in a distant lineal time system but were instead located to the present. Roko-te-whatu, which was The Neck on Lake Hawea, stood as Pokuku's ancestors.

In 1898, my great-grandmother sat at the bedside of her grandfather, Rawiri Te Maire, to record many of the landmarks recited by Wi Pokuku. Rawiri Te Maire saw and understood the hinterland of the South Island in the same manner that his relation Wi Pokuku understood it. So, to answer the question What do Māori see when they look at the natural world? They see their ancestors.

When Wi Pokuku journeyed up the Waitaki Valley to hunt woodhens and to dry eel in the summer, he saw his ancestor Te Rakitamau, or Mount Cuthbert, who would point his way into the Hawea-Wanaka region, where these ancestors were assembled. In an attempt to explain the notion that these ancestors had become mountains, Pokuku's colleague said, "*Ko enei iwi, he iwi inaianei kua wairuatia, kua atua hoki*" (These people have become spirits and gods). But just as important, the *wairua* (spirit) of these ancestors had created the *mauri* (essence) of the South Island, and the *mauri* is best understood as the spiritual life of the land.

As deferential as Elsdon Best was when he said that he did not have insight into the hidden *pa* of knowledge, he had enough insight to understand the idea of *mauri* that so dominates the relationship of Māori to the natural world. *Mauri* is best understood as the spirit of the ancestors within a person or a thing, such as a rock, a bend in a river, or a tree near a house. On a larger scale, our people located their *mauri* for the island within the mountains and rivers. Elsdon Best (in *Maori Religion and Mythology,* Part II, published in 1982) explained the relationship between the *mauri* of a person and the *mauri* of an object as follows. "The material *mauri* representing a person may, according to Tuta Nihoniho, be a stone or a piece of wood. Its power to protect man is implemented in it by the ritual of the priestly adept who locates the *wairua* (spirit or soul) of the defunct parents or ancestors of the person in the material *mauri.* These implanted spirits are the real protecting power, the stone or other object being their temporary abiding place while protecting their living descendant."

For Ngāi Tahu, the *mauri* of the land rested with our ancestors and was sanctified by our high priests, who instilled it in the land, in particular the mountains. And the importance of these ancestral mountains as possessing the *mauri* of the land was evident during the colonization when agents of the British Crown sought to purchase the South Island. Our ancestors were quite clear that they would agree to ceding only the plains from the coastline to the foothills. The mountains, the space where our *mauri* rested, were not to be sold. When Matiaha Tiramōrehu was called to give evidence on what land was ceded to the Crown in 1848, he was clear in his evidence that Ngāi Tahu elders were definitive in saying: "'Let the boundary be from [the mountains] Maungatere to Maungaatua.' That statement gave rise to a long discussion. It was the Maoris who proposed a boundary between the mountains Maunga-tere and Maunga-atua."

Mountains were understood to be *atua* (gods) carried to Te Wai Pounamu upon our canoes to their new homeland from Hawaiki. The Southern Alps that ran as a backbone down the South Island represented our ancestors. Within them rested the *mauri* of the land and the tribe.

So where does this leave us? With a land replete with the spirits of our ancestors that stands in silence? For Māori, the land is not silent and is always speaking. It is this voice that I want to consider, and how it shaped our people. Māori scholarship stands and falls on our oral traditions, and for many of us, our ancestors' chants and incantations are not only beautiful compositions to be heard and appreciated but sources that provide insight into their world and the epiphanies that they experienced, which is why we value them.

The Mountains Speak and Lightning Flashes

The question that follows is How did the *atua* (gods) and *tīpuna* (ancestors), or the mountains, trees, and clouds, speak to our people? And equally important, how did we listen? The terms "nature" and "environment" are impersonal, and I am not all that confident that our people spoke about environmental matters when they spoke about Papatūānuku, the earth mother, and the established pantheon of kin gods, such as Takaroa, the ocean father, or even Tāne, the *atua* of all living things. What we do know is that when our people looked at the earth, they saw an eternal mother that spoke, and when they looked at the Southern Alps, they saw a range of ancestors. What they did not see when speaking to a mountain was the result of tectonic plate movement. The relationship, therefore, is between the people and their *atua* and their ancestors. More specifically, for Māori at least, the relationship was between themselves, their mothers and fathers, their grandmothers and grandfathers, who had passed. It was for the tribal priests to sacredly instill the dead into an object, whether it was a tree or a bend in the river or a bird or other animal, to act as a spiritual guardian.

A whole range of literary scholars have been fascinated by the idea of a sacred geography. The idea can be traced, in particular, to the philosopher Mircia Eliade and his publication *The Sacred and Profane* onward to Joseph Campbell and even to Simon Schama and his magnificent *Landscape and Memory.* Eliade made the point that humans are essentially spiritual beings who seek meaning in their lives. One way in which this is done is by the demarcation of space between the sacred and the profane, and within this space is the center, which he called the "axis-mundi." The axis mundi can be a temple or a hearth within a home, but in the landscape, Eliade tells us, mountains often take the role of the sacred center for early cultures.

Karen Armstrong brings this idea to readers today. In her publications *The Great Transformation* and *A History of Jerusalem,* Armstrong makes the important point that long before people began to map the world scientifically, they had created a "sacred geography" to define their place in the world both emotionally and spiritually. This approach went "far deeper than a cerebral level of the mind." Often sacred beings were associated with the natural world, with the sun, winds, snow, forests, riverways, or mountains. "Anything that stood out from its surroundings and ran counter to the natural order could be a hierophany, a revelation of the divine. A rock or a valley that was particularly beautiful or majestic might indicate the presence of the sacred because it could not be easily fitted into its surroundings. Its very appearance spoke of *something else*." Mountains are an obvious example of a landmark that many ancient cultures regarded as places of the divine, places of transcendence. Early ancestors and mythic heroes climbed to their summits, where they felt they could communicate with their gods because they were midway between heaven and earth. Armstrong explains how Mount Zion would have stood out dramatically from the surrounding hills in a way that seemed to embody the sacred "other," which would later become "holy" (*Jersualem*, pp. 298, 318).

The key point to understand is that these ideas or beliefs were not worked out first and then applied to a particular site, which was then known as a *wahi-tapu*, a sacred land or a holy site. Instead, these beliefs were attempts to explain an experience people felt in a "sacred grove or a mountain peak." Such experiences were then explained in the language of myth, a language of metaphor and symbol. Within this realm of thought was the belief that extraordinary events in nature— lightning, a sun shower, other phenomena—were also associated with the divine. These signs were understood to be examples of the spiritual world attempting to communicate with the living.

Even a casual run through our oral traditions reveals how our ancestors believed features such as mountains, rivers, and trees actively engaged with them at an intimate level. The song that follows was composed in the nineteenth century by a chief, Pāpāhia of the Te Rarawa tribe, Hokianga, Northland. In this song, Pāpāhia learns of the death of his brother, Te Huhu (also known as Te Whārō) from a flash of lightning across the mountain Tauwhare.

> *Tera te uira e hiko i te rangi,*
> *E wahi rua ana ra runga o Tauwhare,*
> *Kaore ia nei ko te tohu o te mate.*
> *Unuhia noatia te ata o Wharo.*
> *I haere wareware ko te hoa i ahau*

> The lightning flashes in the sky,
> Splitting in twain over Tauwhare,
> Assuredly a token of death.
> The shadow of Te Wharo has been withdrawn.
> My friend, forgotten by me, has departed.
>
> (Ngata and Jones, *Ngā Mōteatea,* part I)

Here, the mountain—Tauwhare—is seen to be speaking to the composer, Pāpāhia, by way of lightning, telling him that his relation, Te Whārō, had died. Another equally well-known chant from the Ngā Ruahine people of Taranaki tells of the attack made against the British redoubt on Te Morere—a hillock now known as Sentry Hill. As with the earlier chant, lightning flashes over the peak of Turamoe.

> *E hiko ra e te uira i tai ra,*
> *Kapo taratahi ana te tara ki Turamoe.*
> *Nau mai Tawera e, te whetu kai marama,*
> *Ko te tohu o te mate i tukua ake nei.*

> Lightning flashes on the coastline,
> Flashing upon the peak of Turamoe.
> Venus, the star that eats the moon, the sign of defeat,
> An omen of death sent to ponder.
>
> (Smith, *Taranaki Waiata Tangi,* p. 131)

What becomes apparent is that the world was replete with signs that represented the voice of the *atua*. Stars were obvious representations of our dead but were also seen as omens for battle. If the star Tāwera (Venus) was seen drawing close to the moon, it was said to be "biting the moon," which was seen as an attack against a fort or a tribe. In the chant that follows the composer, Puhi-rawaho, refers to the defeat that fell upon the Waikato tribes in the year 1822.

> *Takiri ko te ata,*
> *Ka ngau Tawera,*
> *Te tohu o te mate,*
> *I huna nga iwi*
> *Ka ngaro ra e*

> Breaks the Dawn
> And Tawera is biting (the moon)
> 'Tis the dread omen of death
> In the annihilation of the tribes
>   (Ngata and Jones, *Ngā Mōteatea*, part II)

The seriousness with which these messages were studied should not be underestimated. As this chant shows, ignoring these signs was foolish.

> *Tera te whetu,*
> *Kamokamo ana mai;*
> *Ka tangi te whatitiri,*
> *Ka rapa te uira,*
> *Te tohu o Hoturoa.*
> *I maunu atu ai;*
> *Kaitoa, kia mate.*

See, the star scintillates in the distance;
The thunder peals, the lightning flashes,
A sign that he of Hoturoa's line is gone.
It serves you right to die!
                    (Ngata and Jones, *Ngā Mōteatea,* pp. 180–181)

The messages did not deal only with the tragic. They also
addressed matters of domestic and seasonal change. For Māori,
the seasonal year commenced with the appearance of Matariki,
the Pleiades constellation. In the chant that follows, a woman
gazes at Matariki and "listens" to its news.

Tirohia atu nei ka whetu rangitia
Matariki, te whetu o te tau
E homai ona rongo kia ako mai atu nei
Ka mate nei au i te matapouri . . .

I gaze upon the stars that shine,
The Pleiades, our stars that mark the year.
The constellation sending me their news and tidings,
rousing my emotions and causing me to reflect
As I dwell here, gloomy and shrouded in sadness . . .
                    (R Tau, Archives, Private Manuscript)

In the South Island, the principal constellation was Puaka,
Orion's Belt. Our ancestors simply noted: "*Kei te Mātahi o Pūaka*
te hoki katoa ai ka tagata ki roto ki kā pā tū mou" (When the new
year started with Puaka, all the people would return home to
their main villages).

Nor was the communication one way. In the South Island,
our ancestors instructed their descendants to openly greet and
acknowledge the constellation Scorpio, *Te Waka a Tamarereti,*

which in our tradition was an ancestral canoe. One tribal elder, Herewini Ira, instructed his descendants thus:

Tā te Māori kī mihi, ka kite ia Tamarereti i te rangi,
ara, tātai whetū ko taua waka tēna.

According to our people, when you see the constellation Tamarereti in the night sky, be aware that it is the canoe and acknowledge it with your greetings.

(R Tau, Archives, Private Manuscript)

It was not only the land that spoke to our people. For Māori the voice of the *atua* was carried by wildlife and in the trees and vegetation. Lizards were often regarded with caution. A proverb associated with them goes, "*Kia kitea, he aitua, he kupapa tahuri*"(When seen, it is an evil omen; disaster follows). The morepork owl was traditionally seen as a messenger from the dead because it appears in the twilight, at the division between the world of Tāne and all living things and that of Tāne's counterpart, his daughter, Hine-nui-te-pō, who took the dead with her into the darkness.

What we have seen so far is that there was an intimate connection between the natural world and the inner world of our ancestors. Unusual natural phenomena were seen to be ancestral voices. This was a world where mountains spoke and the wind carried messages from another realm. This idea is best seen in the North Island term for mountains, Maunga Korero— "Ancestral Mountains That Speak." The signs and voices defined the culture and minds of the community, just as the cultural framework our ancestors created defined the environment. To fully understand the relationship between culture and the environment, we need to set aside the idea that one came before the other. The idea that the environment determined our culture is correct inasmuch as our ancestors saw the environment as containing *atua*—which of course they had created and imposed on it. So when we speak about the natural world as a world of *tohu*—of signs and omens and the voices of our ancestors—we do so because the mechanism in which our ancestors framed, ordered, and categorized the world was complex and tightly bound by the one principle that binds Māori society together: *whakapapa*, a complex network of genealogy.

The environment that our ancestors lived within was an environment of kinship. That kinship was held together by a genealogical web traced not only vertically from Rangi, the sky father, and Papatūānuku, the earth mother, but also horizontally, because Māori did not configure time in a lineal fashion from past to future. Rather, they saw a continual present.

Hinengaro: The Mind of Our People

So far we have seen how our ancestors engaged with the landscape and how the landscape spoke to our people. But this exchange of information, whether the information goes inward or outward, simply brings us to the gap that Best spoke of when he referred to "the outer palisades of the hidden *pa* of knowledge." Information leaves the *pā*, inasmuch as our culture and our ancestors were being imposed on the landscape, and at the same time information comes into the *pā* in the way of *tohu* (signs) from the landscape—in particular, the voices of our ancestors. What we do not have is an explanation of what happens with this information deep inside the *pā*.

At this stage, we need to pause the metaphor used by Best and clarify what he meant. When Best spoke of the hidden pa, he was speaking about the mind of the Māori, and it is the mind of our ancestors we now need to understand.

The first point to understand is that the idea of the
mind existing in the brain is a modern notion that we can
date to the early nineteenth century. Earlier cultures, such as
that of Ancient Greece, often referred to thoughts and actions
emerging from central body parts, maybe the heart, liver, or
intestines.

For Māori and our Polynesian ancestors, the mind was
located in three organs in the midriff. The primary organ was
the *hinengaro* (spleen). The other two organs were the *ngākau*
(intestines) and the *manawa* (heart). Specifically, the *hinengaro* was seen by our ancestors as the seat of the thoughts and
emotions, but the difference between the three organs was a
matter of degree.

Elsdon Best was quite aware of how Māori understood
the mind, and this was evident in an article published in 1901
in the *Journal of the Polynesian Society,* entitled "Spiritual Concepts of the Maori." The article deals with the principal ideas
and beliefs of what we would now call mind and spirit. In it,
Best recorded how the Tuhoe elders from the North Island
outlined the interplay between the spleen, the intestines, and
the heart.

Best tends to decribe all three body parts as the area where
thoughts and emotions are generated. The heart, he writes, is
"the origin and seat of all knowledge, power, intellectuality, it
is the origin of mental and physical strength, it imparts strength
to the *ngakau* [spleen] to love or hate." However, *ngakau*, he
suggests, means "bowels, viscera, and also the heart"; it includes
the other organs individually and collectively as the seat of affection. Best goes on to say, "With the Maori the stomach is the
seat of anger. The *ngakau* is the seat of affection, of mental
pain, of thought." The difference between these states is really
a matter of degree, because they describe emotional states: how
the body feels. More important, these states correspond to what

we now understand to be the mind. For these people the mind was not separated from the body. In other words, our traditions run counter to the Cartesian notion that grew in the West and has dominated much of our thinking up to the present: the idea that the mind exists outside the body. The dualism of mind and body is directly countered by our oral traditions, which say that the body and the mind are one. But our ancestors believed that the body, mind, and the outer world may also have been one.

One of the best explanations of the relationship between Māori and how they felt and thought comes from an account written by Matutaera (Tuta) Nihoniho, who was born in 1850 on the East Coast of New Zealand to the Ngāti Porou tribe, although he later lived in Tuahiwi, in the South Island, where he married into a local family. Nihoniho fought with the government in what are known as the East Coast Wars, which ran from the 1860s to the early 1870s. In 1913, Nihoniho wrote a paper, *Narrative of the Fighting on the East Coast,* that gave advice to his younger kin on the methods of bush warfare. What immediately engages the reader's attention is the extent to which the actions and thoughts of Māori going into battle were defined by their *atua* (gods) speaking to them in a language of *tohu,* signs or omens that came from their inner selves or from their environment. The best way to understand *tohu* is that it is a language of signs. The signs were unusual phenomena that happened in the natural world or within the interior of the person. Lightning, the flowering of trees out of season, an odd gust of wind, or logs drifting against the tide were all seen as manifestations of the divine.

For Māori, all persons have a *wairua,* a spirit that exists within, but it can also travel and communicate with the dead when the person is asleep. In Māori thought, once a person has died, the *wairua* becomes an *atua,* a god, and the prime engagement between *atua* and the living is through dreams. Nihoniho's explanation in his paper starts with an intriguing comparison between the internal world of our ancestors and the external world (my translation):

> *Tuatahi o nga tohu hei tirohanga; ko nga whakahae-*
> *re o nga mahi, me nga ahuatanga o te tangata i nga*
> *awatea; ko nga whakahaere o nga mahi me nga mo-*
> *emoea o te po; e kiia nei e te Tuaiho—E puaki mai*
> *ana te reo o tena rangi, o tena rangi, e whakaatu mo-*
> *hiotanga mai ana hoki tena po, tena po.*

> We first investigate the omens or signs when organizing daily activities and the behavior of man in the light of day and their conduct in the night including one's dreams; because as our distant ancestors have said—voices or messages will come each day and each night wisdom will be revealed.

Connections like the ones Nihiniho describes can be found over and over again with our people. Further into his text, Nihoniho writes: "Study carefully the subject of twitching (*tamaki*, convulsive starts, as of muscles of the limbs and body). If your arm or arms, your leg or legs, or your head be jerked or thrown outward from the body, you at once call out to your companions, 'O friends! I have had a *tamaki.*' Whereupon they will inquire, 'In which direction?' You may reply, 'Toward the mountain yonder.' Then your companions will remark, 'Our enemy is at that place.'"

These twitchings were not random events without meaning, as we would say today. In a tribal world, unusual phenomena such as convulsions were interpreted as signs (*tohu*) from the gods. Nihoniho is very clear on this matter. "These signs do not appear at random: it is only the prompting of Tū-ka-riri and Tū-ka-nguha that causes such manifestations." For Māori, the gods Tū-ka-riri and Tū-ka-nguha are aspects of the war god, Tū, so Tū-ka-riri represents Tū-of-anger, and Tū-ka-nguha, Tū-of-rage. It is here that Nihoniho makes an important point that establishes a connection to the *atua* and the mind: *atua* do not appear simply as natural phenomena but also exist as human phenomena. In other words, the *atua* defined thought and action. Once we understand that the mountains and the external world itself were a world of *atua,* our understanding of the Māori and Polynesian relationship with the natural world fundamentally changes.

When Nihoniho says that the twitching and convulsions of the body were signs of the war god, Tū, he was also saying that the *atua* were present inside the person. This belief was particularly the case with warfare, and there are countless traditions that refer to the presence of *atua* when an erection appears before or during battle. One Māori scholar (quoted in Te Rangihiroa, *The Coming of the Maori,* 1949) wrote: "If the leader of a war party awoke with an erection on the morning before battle, it showed that his courage ran high and hence was regarded as an omen of success." Nihoniho also tells his people that when a war party sets off, they must always watch for the signs of their *atua,* Uenuku, who often appears as a rainbow. If Uenuku appeared behind the war party, then victory was certain. If, however, the rainbow appeared across the path to the enemy, that was a sure sign not to proceed and to retire. Nihoniho again says: "Look carefully at your ancestor Uenuku, who will urge you on or restrain you. Should he be seen by you standing in the form of a [rain]bow over the track behind you as you face your enemy, go on, for that is the time when your enemy will be delivered into your hand by the god."

Similar instructions are given for the different forms of lightning and what they mean.

An equivalent view of the location of the mind seems to have existed throughout the Pacific. In Samoa, the *finagalo*, which is equivalent to *hinengaro*, was understood to be "a chief's will, or desire; to will; . . . a chief's heart, or the seat of the affections." In E. Tregear's *Maori-Polynesian Comparative Dictionary* (1891), *finagalo* is defined as "the liver of a pig or shark. Cf. *finagaloa*, to be angry (of chiefs)." But, like the Māori language, Samoan also uses the word *manava* (*manawa* in Māori) to explain the idea of having different opinions. Its variant *manatu* refers to "a thought" but also means "to think" and "to remember." The *manava* is located in the belly, but it is also the word for a child's fontanel.

The Tahitian language is similar in that *manawa* is again located in the belly, specifically the "interior man," as Tregear points out. He translates *manava* as "the belly, the stomach; . . . the interior man," and refers to a variant, *Manavanava*, which means "to think, to ponder." Likewise, in Hawai'i *manawa* is understood to mean "feelings, affection, sympathy." Tregear makes further comparisons: "Cf. *mana*, spirit, energy, intelligence; *manao*, to think; *mananao*, thought, opinion; *manawanui*, patience; steadfast in difficulties."

A fairly reasonable conclusion would be that the mind is not what we think it is but what we feel it is, but I do not think this summary does justice to how our ancestors configured their world. Our traditions tell us that when our ancestors looked at the land, the ocean, and the stars and when they felt the wind, they felt, saw, and heard their ancestors. When they journeyed across Polynesia, they took their ancestors and planted them upon the land, and those ancestors spoke to our people in *tohu*, whether in lightning that flashed or flowers that blossomed out of season.

Just as our ancestors spoke from the mountains, they also spoke in our dreams and through the twitching of our bodies. All of these voices were *tohu* of our *atua* speaking to us. The difference between our ancestors speaking from a mountain or in a dream was only a matter of degree. The implications are substantial, but we need to avoid engaging in Western logic by arguing that our people were unable to escape the reflections of their ancestors, their traditions, or themselves: that they believed the gods controlled all thought. Yet any reader of our history understands that the world of our ancestors was anything but lineal and that it would be a mistake to think the *atua* controlled all thought, because our *hinengaro* (spleens, minds) also controlled the *atua*.

Just as Matiaha drew the *atua* into his world in the winter of June 1849, Māori also removed the *atua* from their world. One of the more interesting chants of our people is the chant to remove the *atua* (my translation).

Wetea mai te whiwhi	Unravel the knots that bind
Wetea mai te hara	Unravel offense
Wetea mai te tapu	Unravel the sacred
Wetea ra pea kia mawetewete	Unravel to allow one to be free
Wetea ra pea kia mataratara	Unravel to allow one to be free from entanglement
Tawhiti te rangi ka taea nga tapu	The heavens are distant and the *tapu* of the gods can be overcome

This is an incantation to unravel oneself from controlling *atua*, to be free from the sacred, the *tapu*. We know from our traditions that although the *atua* are eternal, their spirit, or *wairua*, is not

immortal. Our traditions tell us that our ancestors are in continual confrontation with their *atua* and that the relationship is
not one of supplication as we find in the West. Māori do not
pray to their *atua;* rather, they invoke them to confront and
engage; the relationship is dynamic. Our ancestors place themselves almost alongside the *atua,* always contesting them, always
seeking a balanced relationship.

Our people were continually challenging the *atua,* just as
the *atua* and the environment challenged them. We can see this
relationship in two places. The first is in the incantations that
high priests used throughout the Pacific to fell a tree, whether
it was for a canoe or a house. The chant that follows is known
throughout the Pacific in different variations. It tells of the
story of Rata (or Laka, as he is known in Hawai'i), who felled
a tree only to find the tree standing again in the morning. Rata
had failed to engage the *atua* through the proper rituals and
incantations, including the *atua* Tāne—the tree. Once he had
learned the rituals and the way to engage with the *atua,* his
incantation ran as follows (my translation). It possibly represents the high point of Māori oratory.

Ko te tuanga o te rakau ki raro	For the felling of a tree
Kakariki Powhaitere	My incantation goes to the Parakeets
I te wao-nui-a-Tāne	Of Tāne's Great Forest
I te Urunga tapu	The sacred resting place
Kua ara kua ara	Where Tāne was
A Tāne ki runga	Raised above
Kua kotia nga putake	The base of the trees set aside for

Te rakau o te whare nei	The meetinghouse have been cut.
Kua waiho atu	They have been left
I te Urunga tapu	In the sacred resting place.
Kua kotia nga kauru	The head of the tree set aside for
Te whare o te rakau nei	The meetinghouse has been cut
Kua waiho atu	And has been set aside in
I te wai-nui-a-Tāne	Tāne's Great Forest.
Kua tae au	I have gone
Ki nga pukenga	To the high priests
Ki nga Wananga	To those with knowledge
Ki nga tauira	And to those who learn
Patua kuru	My mallet has been struck
Patua whao	My chisel has been struck
Patua te toki a Taiharuru	The adze of the seas
Kua piki hoki nei	Of Tangaroa has struck
Ki te maro hukahuka-nui	And the crests of the waves
A Tangaroa	Climb higher
Te Ngaru ai e whati ai	To obstruct and break
E nuku-Tai-maroro	Against the canoe, Nuku-tai-maroro
Kaore ko au ko Rata	I am not Rata.
E kimi ana e hahau ana	I search and seek
I nga uri o te whanau a Rata	The descendants of Rata's family
Hai pokapoka i a Tāne	So as to carve the Tree of Tāne
E tu i-i-i	That stands before me
Kaore i kitea	I do not see them

Kua mate noa atu	As they died
I te awa Piko-Piko-i-Whiti	At the river Pikopiko-i-whiti
Ma te maranga mai ai	It is their spirits that I ask to rise and stand with me in this ritual
Ko Hiku nuku e	As the heavens separate
Ta taua rangi.	And aid me on this sacred day.

The Tainui version states, "*Kaore ko au ko Rata, E kimi ana, e hahau ana, I te awa i Pikopiko-i-whiti.*" This would read, "I am not Rata. I seek and search for you on the river Pikopiko-i-whiti." This line clarifies the notion that the priest seeks the aid of Rata.

Rata recites his incantation to the parakeets of the forest, who were the spirits and descendants of Tāne, the god of the forest, humankind, and all living things. Once the trunk had been set aside, he then informs the *atua* that he has formally learned the required rituals. Rata says that he has learned from the priests and within the formal schools of learning. Therefore, he uses his adze to strike Tāne, the tree. The point to note is that the adze he uses is the "adze of the seas of Tangaroa." In Māori thought, Tāne and Tangaroa are *atua* always in opposition, and the actual stone used is a creation of Tangaroa, *atua* of the ocean. Here, the striking of the adze on the tree is compared to the crashing of the waves against the land and against Tāne's descendants. Our people believed that Tangaroa and Tāne—the *atua* of the ocean and the forest—opposed each other. To fell the tree of Tāne, Māori invoked Tangaroa and his adze.

At the end, the tribal priest who recites the incantation declares he is not Rata but that he seeks and searches for him where he rests back in the homeland of Hawaiki so he can stand by his side as he fells the tree. This is not a prayer of supplication. It is an invocation of ancestors and *atua* to stand as god against god.

This is the meaning behind the well-known rhetorical question asked by Māori in their oratory on *marae* or in *mote-atea* (prose, oral arts) and *haka* (aggressive, defiant perfor-mances): *"He tangata, he tipua, he atua ranei?"* (Are you a man, a demigod, or a god?). In part this question is really a challenge wherein Māori will ask their opponents whether they are just human or something greater. The answer for Māori is that we are all of these. One of the more significant explanations of sacredness is found in our manuscripts, wherein an elder (quoted in J. White's *Miscellaneous Manuscripts* of 1887) declares:

> *Na Tane ano te tapu, i kimihia e ia ki te waho (wao ngahere) nui o Tane.*

> Tapu belongs to Tane and it was found by him in the Great Forest of Tane.

Tane (*Tāne*) is shorthand for "man." In other words, we create our gods just as we create the environment.

This brings us back to the beginning of this chapter. Elders such as Matiaha Tiramōrehu had learned in their traditional schools of learning that the posts of their ancestors were smeared with blood to give them life. When Rata felled the tree for a meetinghouse or when the carved pillars in the house were revived with the spirit of ancestors, the difference between a tree, a rock, or a meetinghouse was slight. As the passage above tells us, it was the high priests who made these things sacred or otherwise. The environment was not limited to nature, because it also included what archaeologists would call material objects. Māori would also include technology. In 1827, the artist Augus-tus Earle, who sailed from New Zealand to Australia with Māori, recorded their excitement when they saw their first windmills as their brig anchored: "Nothing could exceed the delight manifested by our New Zealanders as we sailed up Port Jackson [Sydney] harbour; but above all, the windmills most astonished them. After dancing and screaming with joy at beholding them, they came running and asking me, 'if they were not gods'" (quoted in F. Hanson and L. Hanson, *Counterpoint in Māori Culture*). A similar observation was made earlier in 1823 by Captain Edwardson of the sloop *Snapper* when he noted the connection Māori made between *Pakeha* (White people) and the material objects they carried with them: "The beautiful and curious articles which they see in the hands of the Europeans make them regard the latter as a species of devils or spirits, heetouas [*atua*]" (quoted in R. McNab, *Murihiku*).

The reason these references are made is that we need to assess what is meant by environment in the same way we need to assess what we mean by the mind, at least when we are dealing with a culture that is vastly different from Western culture. If we are going to speak about what our Pacific ancestors thought when dealing with the environment, we should examine not only what we mean by "thought" but also what we mean by "environment."

The word we use today for the environment is *taiao*, but it properly refers to the world or to a particular part of a country or district. For our people, a tree and a carved pillar were both living beings.

It would be very easy to argue that as Māori settled a new island in a vastly different landscape, their identity and thinking as a people changed as their ways of living changed. But this was not the case. When Captain James Cook arrived in New Zealand on the *Endeavour* in 1769 with the priest Tupaia of Raiatea, Tupaia was able to communicate with our people. As Joseph Banks wrote at Tologa Bay on October 25: "Went ashore this morn and renewd our searches for plants &c. with great success. In the mean time Tupia who staid with the waterers

had much conversation with one of their preists; they seemd
to agree very well in their notions of religion only Tupia was
much more learned than the other and all his discourse was
heard with much attention. He askd them in the course of his
conversation with them many questions, among the rest
whether or no they realy eat men which he was very loth to
beleive; they answered in the affirmative saying that they eat
the bodys only of those of their enemies who were killed in war"
(quoted in W. P. Worrell, *Sir Joseph Banks in New Zealand*). We
know that our people had departed from their homeland of
Hawaiki almost 700 years before Cook's arrival in New Zealand,
roughly between 1100–1200. We also know that the people who
settled New Zealand came from East Polynesia, Tupaia's homeland. Yet despite the gap in time, Banks's account shows that
Tupaia was able to communicate with our priests on tribal
customs "with much attention."

The example of Tupaia is one that Kanaka Maoli of
Hawai'i, Māohi of Tahiti, and Māori of New Zealand understand, nor did engagement stop with Tupaia and our ancestors
of Tologa Bay. It has been repeated over the centuries. Our
ancestors throughout the Pacific thought and saw the world in
much the same way. There was little difference between Kanaka Maoli, Māohi, and Māori. From these traditions, we can also
draw conclusions about the relationship between our ancestors,
the environment, and the way we thought and felt.

When our people saw the environment, they saw their
ancestors and engaged with them as such. Our traditions show
us that the mind and the body are one and the same, that there
is no separation between the two. But I expect we can extend
this to suggest that our ancestors did not separate their *hinengaro* from the environment. In fact, an actual separation
between one's *hinengaro* and the environment would have

been just as unthinkable as a separation of the *hinengaro* from the body.

Here I am deliberately using *hinengaro* instead of "mind,"' because we can locate the *hinengaro* within the body; the mind we cannot. Clearly, *atua* are cultural impositions upon the land, which is evident when we accept that our ancestors saw little difference between a tree, a mountain, a canoe, and, as Augustus Earle tells us, windmills.

From a Māori perspective, a question worth asking is whether the Western separation of environment, mind, and culture is any different from the Māori way of thinking about the three. The mind in Western thought is more ghostly than the *hinengaro* because it cannot be located with any certainty, so it is worth asking whether the mind is really culture. Māori created and imposed their '*atua*' upon the world, which in turn spoke to them. Does that mean that culture is a secular way Western society imposes its gods upon the world? Is there much difference between Western and Māori views?

This path of thought is tempting, not least because Western thought has often been used to evaluate Māori worldviews. While turnabout is fair play (and appealing as an exercise), would it be productive? Best, quoted at the beginning of the chapter, certainly realized that he could not look at the world as the Māori did, despite his vast knowledge of the people and their language and culture. Is looking at Western thought from a Māori perspective likely to be more rewarding than looking at Māori thought from a Western perspective? In both cases, it may be more rewarding to stand shoulder to shoulder and look at the world together, to seek the insights that each worldview can develop, than to stand face to face and seek to evaluate each other's perspectives.

8

Similarities and Differences in Island Social-Environmental Systems

Peter M. Vitousek, Kawika B. Winter, and
Kamanamaikalani Beamer

The clarity with which the development of social-environmental systems can be evaluated in Polynesian island societies, and the manner in which this has been documented in two different knowledge systems, Polynesian and Western, is unique, as demonstrated in the foregoing chapters. The further differentiation of cultures in the context of a shared Polynesian identity is fascinating. In this chapter we will explore the drivers of this differentiation, which led to distinct social-environmental systems, and the forces that maintained a collective meta-culture. We begin with the core similarities of the founding societies of each island. (Tikopia is an exception. There, later Polynesian voyagers came to dominate an earlier society that drew heavily on the tools and biota of nearby Near Oceanic islands.)

Perhaps the most obvious set of similarities in founding cultures can be seen in the Polynesian languages. The words used to describe resources, technologies, and the social structures that surrounded them—*kalo/taro* (taro), *'uala/kumara* (sweet potato), *ali'i/ariki* (hereditary chief), *wa'a/waka/vaka* (canoe)—are evidence of this shared founding culture. Another set of similarities can be seen in the suite of plants—taro, sweet potato, yam, banana/plantain, breadfruit, gourd, candlenut, barkcloth, all transported to islands by the Polynesian discoverers—that not only provide food and material culture but are vehicles for stories that convey concepts of shared identity and morality through the generations.

The systems developed to cultivate these plants reflect both similarities and differences, as would be expected in the development of social-environmental systems. Cropping systems were developed to operate within the constraints of islands in the largest ocean on the planet, an ocean that—from an Indigenous perspective—tied people together rather than separated them. Ingenuity allowed Polynesians to take advantage of the opportunities presented by the broad array of ecological conditions on very different islands to sustainably provide for their needs in very different situations. Of the animals that Polynesians introduced to Pacific islands, rats in particular have been the cause of irreparable ecological harm, which has been another recurring theme in Pacific islands; still, the ways in which Polynesians managed to live sustainably for centuries within island environments plagued by ecosystem-altering invasive species are nothing short of amazing.

People applied their ideas, technologies, and biocultural toolkits of introduced plants and animals to transform their new lands, often by seeking to establish the production systems of their ancestral homelands. In some cases, Hawai'i for example, the Indigenous systems worked in their new lands—

notably in the highly productive and sustainable *loʻi kalo* (taro paddies), cropping systems in the discoverers' homelands that were developed further in parts of Hawaiʻi. These wetland systems were coupled with agroforestry practices that maintained the ecosystem services that forests provide while increasing food production. The systems were so energy efficient—measured as a ratio of caloric and nutritional needs of cultivators to caloric and nutritional output to society—and materially productive that in many regions they provided Hawaiians with a surplus that gave them the time, energy, and resources to focus on the development of arts (such as dance and featherwork) and to emphasize sports (such as year-round surfing and an annual archipelago-wide season of games).

In many cases, however, it was clear to newly migrated Polynesians that their new lands would not support their traditional ways of obtaining food, and in other cases they sought to establish ancestral systems but ultimately abandoned them. Evidence of the latter situation exists in the recently discovered remains of wetland taro cultivation on Ahuahu (Great Mercury Island) in Aotearoa. Whether the settlers saw initially that ancestral systems would not work or whether they tried but ultimately failed to establish such systems (as in the example from Aotearoa above), it would have been clear to them that they needed to develop alternatives. This need to innovate approaches to agroecology was one of the drivers of differentiation because, as Kawika Winter and colleagues described in 2018, a culture's agroecological system is the foundation element upon which a society is built.

The capacity for innovation displayed in the development of alternatives is remarkable, as are the resulting alternative forms of Polynesian production systems and societies. In Hawaiʻi, innovations included new systems for the intensive production of food surpluses in favorable environments—notably the massive rain-fed field systems on fertile soils of the younger islands and aquacultural systems that were adapted to fresh water, brackish water, and salt water. These innovative food systems were developed and sustained within the context of a uniquely Hawaiian approach to ecosystem-based management, using traditional land divisions (*moku*), that ensured the sustainability of a large-scale social-ecological system that spanned the archipelago.

This *moku* system fostered the development of large-scale public works and a high degree of social organization and hierarchy, which led to the initial development of several island-based kingdoms within the archipelago. It was the cumulative ability of these large social-environmental systems to produce material resources, coupled with innovations that concentrated abiotic resources and allowed for sustainable food production in unfavorable environments, that supported armies of tens of thousands of men. These massive armies eventually facilitated the conquest of all the individual island-based kingdoms and their unification into a single kingdom encompassing the entire archipelago.

Examples of innovations can be seen elsewhere as well—as in the rock gardens on Rapa Nui, which (like the rain-fed field systems of the geologically younger islands in Hawai'i) are an alternative social-ecological system that can thrive in areas without perennial streams. The adaptations facilitated intensive production in landscapes that were unsuitable for the development of *lo'i kalo*. The challenge facing the discoverers of Aotearoa was even deeper in that it was the only place colonized by Polynesians that had a temperate climate with a winter season, which was predictably inhospitable to their crops over most of the landscape. A response to these conditions over most of Aotearoa was the development of a system of food storage, together with a unique-to-Polynesia system of forts (*pā*) that protected stored food.

All of these innovations had consequences for the environments within which they were developed, and all of them had ramifications for the societies that developed them. When a well-defined culture and a circular economy—one in which waste products from one process are used as inputs to another process, so that there is little or no waste—was established on very different islands, very different societies resulted and interacted with their islands in a range of different ways. A set of populous and hierarchical nations organized large-scale public works (irrigation systems, rain-fed field systems, marine aquaculture systems) in Hawai'i, well-defined tribes and clans or subtribes organized island-wide trading networks in Aotearoa, an extraordinarily sustainable forest-based agricultural system was developed on Tikopia, and magnificent ceremonial architecture was built on Rapa Nui. Biophysical features of the islands were shaped as well. The forests that regulated water quantity and quality in the *moku* of Hawai'i were protected, but forests were completely lost on Rapa Nui.

In making the point that features of the islands shaped the social-environmental systems of Polynesia, we are not suggesting that the biophysical features of these very different islands determined the societies that emerged; rather, as Patrick Kirch in the Tikopia chapter and Noa Lincoln, Mehana Vaughan, and Natalie Kurashima in the Hawai'i chapter point out, there are many contingencies in the development of any society, and there is no reason to expect the same path to be followed or the same endpoint reached in all interactions between particular founding societies and particular islands, especially if those interactions could take place multiple times. Moreover, features of land and features of culture influence each other in multiple ways, and those influences themselves interact in ways that are difficult to predict. Nevertheless, features of islands do affect features of society, and we believe that even though there is no determinism, there is some regularity, some generality, to those effects.

We do not see anything in the biophysical features of Rapa Nui that led that island's society to develop monumental architecture, or in Tikopia's that led it to develop what is perhaps the most explicitly sustainable production system and population policy on earth (although we agree with Kirch's suggestion in 1997 that the Tikopia could not have done what they did were their island not a relatively young volcanic island with relatively fertile soils). However, we do not think any of the societies considered here other than Hawai'i could have developed into complex, hierarchical kingdoms, nor do we think any of these societies other than those on Aotearoa could have developed the network of fortifications that they did (and that they evolved to employ effectively against colonizers). Hawai'i and Aotearoa might not have followed the paths they did, but none of the other islands' societies could have followed their paths.

When we started writing this book, we believed that the best evidence for the role of land in influencing culture, and the role of both culture and land in influencing the development of social-environmental systems, would come from a comparison of different islands and archipelagoes. Perhaps with a larger sample of islands and societies, that would be true; perhaps with the development of Indigenous scholarship across the Pacific, that analysis will be shown to be the more powerful one at some time in the future. However, for now we have come to believe that the best evidence is to be found by comparisons within rather than between archipelagoes and their societies. These comparisons are particularly apt for the largest islands and archipelagoes in Polynesia, Aotearoa and Hawai'i.

In Hawai'i, groups of Polynesian voyagers came in different waves from the Central Pacific, spread out across the archipelago, intermingled, and developed alternative social-ecological systems in the very different environments across Hawai'i. The societies, which were built upon different foundational agricultural production systems, stand in stark contrast to one another. The people who established a society in the moderately dry district of Kona on the island of Hawai'i had a similar ancestral background to those who established societies in the well-watered districts of Ko'olau and Halele'a on the island of Kaua'i, yet their social-environmental systems were notably distinct. The society that developed on Kona was necessarily different from those that developed in Ko'olau and Halele'a; the abundance of flowing fresh water in those districts of Kaua'i and the richness of the nearshore reef made it relatively simple to produce a substantial surplus of food there. In contrast, people in Kona succeeded in developing a cropping system that produced a surplus, despite the absence of surface water or (in most places) a well-developed coral reef, by using an innovative rain-fed field system of agriculture. There is even evidence that different gods in the Polynesian pantheon were considered more central to the societies in those different areas.

Similarly, the people who established societies in the cold southern part of Te Wai Pounamu (the South Island) were not in their origin distinct from those who established societies in Northland, the subtropical northern part of Te Ika ā Maui (the North Island). Indeed, oral histories make it clear that Ngāi Tahu, now the paramount tribe of most of Te Wai Pounamu, moved there from Te Ika ā Maui well after Māori settlement, and that the tribe defeated, displaced, and partly incorporated two earlier tribes that had been there before their arrival. In southern Te Wai Pounamu, new arrivals discovered (as their predecessors no doubt had) that the cold climate and the short summer season meant that none of their crops, even the fast-growing and short-season sweet potato, could provide food. Of necessity, and no doubt with substantial innovation, they took the unusual step of developing from an agricultural society into a hunting and gathering society, though one that maintained the large-scale organization and trade networks that are more common among agricultural societies.

A comparison of southern Te Wai Pounamu to Northland, or of Kona to Halele'a, is not just a comparison of different lands or different societies that had developed from common origins. Rather, it is a comparison of different social-environmental systems. As the Hawai'i chapter makes clear, the main challenge in both Kona and Halele'a was managing fresh water, but the sources of the fresh water were very different—surface streams in Halele'a, rain in Kona. Consequently, maintaining the upland forest that regulated the quantity and quality of water was an existential challenge—and a cultural and religious imperative—in Halele'a. In Kona, practices that made use of and conserved rain—planting times, mulching practices, the matrix of vegetation and its influence on evaporation—were most important. Both the structure of biophysical systems on the landscape and the social institutions that managed and controlled fresh water (and human labor) differed between these regions—and did so in complex ways that depended on how landscape and cultural institutions interacted, indeed evolved, together. A similar comparison can be made in Aotearoa, where the southern part of Te Wai Pounamu was unsuitable for any Polynesian crops, so societies developed preservation techniques and long-distance trade networks that moved spatially and that temporally constrained resources throughout the landscape. In contrast, much of Aotearoa supported cropping of *kumara* (sweet potato)—but only seasonally—with the imperative (absent in much of Polynesia) for the storage of yields through an unfavorable season for crop growth.

While the environmental influences that landscapes had on societies, and vice versa, is easy to see, the related influence of the biodiversity of culturally important plants upon those landscapes and cultures is less obvious, but perhaps it is equally important; the biodiversity is certainly indicative of cultural similarities and differentiation. A closer look at plant diversity throughout the region provides insight into the nature of the coevolutionary trajectory that each Polynesian culture followed as it developed from its shared origin. All of the Polynesian cultures and identities were shaped by the same core elements of a biocultural toolkit that were culturally foundational to their ancestors in their homelands. Through the course of the Polynesian diaspora each island group managed unique gene pools of these common species (at times subsets of them), and in time each of these gene pools evolved in distinct lineages. The genetic diversity that existed within the suite of crops managed on each island provided the underpinnings for a diversification of culture.

The environment of each island society had constraints that limited which crops could thrive, but these limitations also provided opportunities for diversification of not only cropping systems but also plant genetics. One example is the selection in Tikopia of *pulaka vao* (giant swamp taro) to fit into an upland arboricultural system. Elsewhere, in the islands of Hiva (Marquesas), the lack of deep alluvial soils limited the cultivation of the taro and sweet potatoes that dominated agriculture systems elsewhere in Polynesia. As a result, the Mā'ohi (Indigenous people) shifted focus to the cultivation of breadfruit trees, eventually developing and managing more than 500 distinct cultivars of breadfruit trees in their agroforestry systems. Not surprisingly, they also maintained only limited taro diversity. Conversely, in Hawai'i the broad range of ecological diversity and the presence of deep alluvial soils allowed for intensive cultivation of herbaceous crops, which led to the diversification of hundreds of *kalo* (taro) and *'uala* (sweet potato) cultivars, along with dozens of *mai'a* (banana and plantain) and *kava* (kava) cultivars, but just a single cultivar of *'ulu* (breadfruit).

The focal species for diversification, as well as the manners of diversification, are perhaps the easiest way to assess which crop species were the most important for each Polynesian culture. Knowing them also tells which plants played the central role in the evolution of that culture. Perhaps the most obvious example of this biocultural evolution is seen in language. As Kawika Winter pointed out in 2012, *kānaka* (Native Hawaiians) developed upwards of 400 distinct cultivars of *kalo*. Each of these distinct cultivars was given a name, which increased the linguistic diversity of the Hawaiian language by as many words and marked its distinctiveness from other Polynesian languages. Each new word added to a language constitutes further divergence, in an evolutionary sense, from an undifferentiated ancestral Polynesian language and culture.

However, the evolutionary influence of *kalo* on Hawaiian culture did not stop there. Each of the distinct cultivars had not only its own name but also its own story. Sometimes stories connected directly to the lineage of a family or the history of a community; at other times they conveyed lessons about morality and behavior. Beyond the stories, some of these cultivars were identified as being needed for particular culinary preparations, medicinal applications, or ceremonial offerings. While *kalo* filled a foundational function in Hawaiian society, much as it did in most other Polynesian cultures, and therefore maintained Hawaiian culture as a Polynesian culture, the coevolutionary relationship between Hawaiians and *kalo* contributed to the divergence of Hawaiian culture into a clearly distinctive and yet recognizably Polynesian culture. The diversification of this and other crop species in Hawai'i resulted in hundreds of uniquely Hawaiian words and just as many stories, not to mention the countless contributions this diversification provided to culinary traditions, medicinal applications, and ceremonial practices that existed nowhere else beyond Hawai'i, and thus contributes to identifying Hawaiian culture as unique within Polynesia. The same is true for each of the Polynesian cultures. The evolutionary influence that biodiversity had—and continues to have—on Polynesian cultures should not be understated.

Plants are not only drivers of the diversification of culture; they are also a glue that keeps a core Polynesian identity together. Just as *kalo* varieties were selected and diversified in Hawai'i and as a result contributed to the distinctiveness and diversification of Hawaiian culture, they served the core function of keeping Hawaiian culture a Polynesian culture. The same push and pull between cultural diversification and cultural alignment existed for all of the crop species. Similar dynamics occur for the biodiversity of native species. For example, the genus *Pipturus* exists throughout Polynesia, and certain species have noted medicinal properties. These are called *mamaki* or a related cognate in several Polynesian cultures, and they have been incorporated into agroforestry systems. Thus, *mamaki* is a native species that was found in, rather than introduced to, the islands that Polynesians discovered and settled. It is representative of the elements of landscapes that kept Polynesian cultures together in terms of linguistics, practices, and identity.

Other native species had the opposite effect. Members of the genus *Metrosideros* are hardwood trees found in all of the high islands of Polynesia and are commonly used by Polynesians for carving. In spite of the similar form these trees have and their similar function in both the forests and material Polynesian culture, they have very different names in each of the Polynesian archipelagoes—'ōhi'a lehua in Hawai'i, *laka* in Tahiti, and *pohutukawa* in Aotearoa—and each has a very distinct place-based origin story associated with it. Other unique Aotearoa species of *Metrosideros* are named *rata*, which is cognate to the Tahitian name and to the name of the Hawaiian goddess of the forest. The reasons for the difference between *Pipturus* and *Metrosideros* are not clear, but they are evidence of the roles native plants played both in pushing Polynesian cultures toward diversification and in holding them together. Other features of the biological diversity of islands that Polynesians discovered played a similar role, as did Polynesian-introduced crop species.

The remarkable success of Polynesian exploration and expansion across more than 50 million square kilometers of ocean is an unparalleled achievement in human history. The ability to develop complex and sustainable societies across diverse ecosystems and climate zones was in large part due to the discoverers' intimate relationships with natural systems, which facilitated their development of innovative place-specific food systems. Their connection to natural systems can provide valuable lessons for modern societies.

9
Sustainability in Polynesian Island Societies

Pamela A. Matson, Peter M. Vitousek,
Kamanamaikalani Beamer, and T. Kaeo Duarte

"Sustainability" has taken on so many (positive) meanings to so many communities that there are those who argue that the concept no longer means anything useful. Here we follow a 2016 book by Pamela Matson and colleagues to define sustainability as meaning "intergenerational well-being" or, in a more extended form, "providing for people now and in future generations while protecting the life-support system of the planet." This definition is inherently anthropocentric, as is the concept it represents. In this chapter, we ask if the social-environmental systems that developed on Polynesian islands were sustainable, and to the extent that they were, we ask if the paths that Polynesian societies took toward sustainability could inform our twenty-first-century global society as it attempts to navigate a transition to sustainability.

There are several reasons to expect that Pacific islanders would be more likely than others to build sustainable societies.

One important reason is that they were islanders: their islands were their worlds. As is discussed in the introduction and chapter 1, the isolation of islands to seagoing people like Polynesians can be overstated; nevertheless, it is true that they lived on island worlds; they could see when their activities were filling up their islands; they could see that what was left was all there was or would be. In another sense, Polynesians in the past were people of their time and place. They did not draw resources from all over the world, only from their islands and the surrounding ocean. They did not make use of energy that had been stored in the past (fossil fuels); they did not borrow money from future generations, as modern society does through the use of a discount rate. Society had to function successfully in the present, and in doing so, it could not damage the resource base in a way that made it impossible for future generations to function successfully in their present.

That Polynesians were and are island people predisposed them to the creation of sustainable societies, and at least two other factors might have augmented that predisposition. One that could be important is their view of plants, animals, and features of the environment as kin, often as ancestors and/or *akua/atua* (gods). Kamanamaikalani Beamer (an author of this chapter) used to take Polynesian visitors to *loʻi kalo* (taro paddies) that he developed and worked in; when he did so, he would tell the Hawaiian origin story, in which the sky father and the earth mother, Wākea and Papahānaumokuākea, have a daughter Hoʻohōkūkalani. Wākea and Hoʻohōkūkalani then have a stillborn child, Hāloa, who becomes the corm of *kalo* (taro). Subsequent children of Wākea and Hoʻohōkūkalani give rise to humanity. Kamanamaikalani, a Native Hawaiian, then says, "We are told we migrated here from the southern Pacific—and we did. But when you get into paddies to work, carrying with you the worldview that you are caring for your ancestors, you are mindful of the intimacy of our actions and relationships with *kalo*." Similarly, discussions involving Māori Fellows of the First Nations' Futures Program at Stanford on the topic of human well-being make it clear that determinants of well-being for individual Māori participants go beyond personal factors, such as health, education, access to material needs, security, and the opportunity to choose, to include the health and well-being of the natural systems of the places where they live (which, as chapter 7 makes clear, they view as relatives). They argue that separating human well-being from the well-being of nature is not possible for them. Harming our living systems is harming family, as much as nurturing living systems is essentially nurturing extended family.

The other component of a Polynesian worldview that could contribute to sustainability is the importance of genealogy. Peter Vitousek and Pamela Matson (also authors of this chapter, who are married to each other, have two children, and are not Polynesian) recall a conversation in Aotearoa in which a Māori elder said that family is important to Māori in the same way that money is important to Americans. They were offended, since they regard their family as being much more important to them than money. Further conversation made it clear that they thought they valued their descendants as much as he did his—but they placed much less importance on their ancestors than he did on his. Thinking about that conversation now, Peter and Pamela wonder whether it is possible for them to place as much emphasis on their descendants as he did—excepting their children and their so-far-theoretical children's children—if they don't see their ascendants with the same care that they see their descendants and if they don't see themselves as links in a chain that reaches far back into the past as well as far forward into the future. In essence, in the Polynesian worldview there is a strong and real sensitivity to the influence of time—both backwards and forwards—on one's actions and impacts in the present. As Te Maire Tau points out in chapter 7, Māori did not configure time in a lineal fashion with past, present, and future but saw a continual present.

Thus, it seems logical that viewing the nonhuman world as kin or, indeed, as an inseparable part of being human, made islanders more inclined to take actions that modern societies would regard as sustainable, and that seeing themselves as the present embodiments and links in a lineage that stretched back many generations and would reach forward for many generations in the place where they lived made them more inclined to take a long-term perspective that led to more sustainable societies. How pertinent is this worldview to the transition to more sustainable living that our globalized twenty-first-century society needs to make? Here we look at the past Polynesian societies discussed in earlier chapters to evaluate when and how they reached toward sustainability and whether their successes or failures in doing so can provide useful lessons that globalized societies could learn.

To frame our discussion, we draw on a broad conceptualization of sustainability that has been used in current global analyses of sustainability and that some of us use in teaching and thinking about sustainability challenges. It is not a grand master plan for sustainability; rather, it is an attempt to identify a common set of elements that influence the ability of societies to meet the needs of their people and support their well-being not just in the near term but across generations. As illustrated in figure 9.1, the framework encompasses the production and provision of goods and services needed to sustain people and meet the goal of human well-being across generations, here posited to ultimately rest on five broad groups of resources or assets that come from nature or are human-made—typically called human, social, natural, manufactured, and

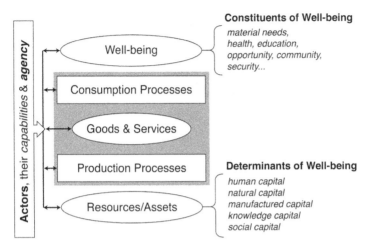

Figure 9.1. A framework for considering sustainability, with intergenerational, inclusive human well-being as the goal of sustainability efforts. Republished with permission of Princeton University Press, from Matson et al., *Pursuing Sustainability*, 2016; permission conveyed through Copyright Clearance Center, Inc.

knowledge capital assets. Figure 9.2 lists examples of important assets that are included in those broad groupings, and table 9.1 clarifies the differences in these resource stocks or assets in the specific case of the current management of ocean fisheries. If those resource stocks or assets are in place, actors in societies (including individuals and organizations with agency to drive decisions and make change) have the potential to do the things that are needed to sustain their communities. If one or more of the assets is degraded or missing, action to sustain people's well-being within and across generations is likely to be undermined.

While our understanding of the dynamics of Polynesian island societies over time may not be sufficient to test the assets framework to the fullest, we can use it to consider the different pathways of three societies discussed in this book: two societies

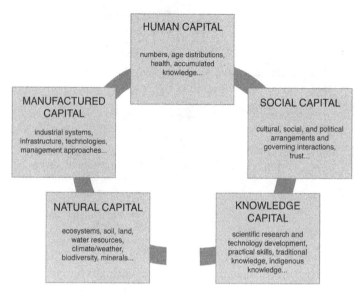

Figure 9.2. Stocks of resources or assets that underpin efforts toward sustainability.

that seem to express alternative pathways toward sustainability (Tikopia and Hawai'i) and one that is widely (if not wholly accurately) treated as a cautionary tale of the consequences of failure to maintain sustainability (Rapa Nui).

The narrative is widespread that the Rapanui people overexploited the limited resources of their island—their natural capital—and so drove an endogenous collapse that changed an organized, surplus-producing society that created monumental architecture into a chaotic society that destroyed that same architecture. This narrative is contested by people who argue that any collapse that occurred had more to do with European contact and colonization, with the concomitant spread of disease and loss of Indigenous capacity (in other words, loss of human capital), than with any internal dynamics of Rapa Nui society,

Table 9.1.   Resource or Asset Stocks That Underpin Human Well-Being

Resource Group	Representative Ocean Fishery Stocks	Representative Resource Stocks
Natural Capital		
Ecosystems	fish and their food	biota, biomass, communities
Environment	ocean temperature, pH	climate, quantity and quality of land, air, water
Minerals	fossil fuel for fishing boats	fossil fuels, iron, sand, etc.
Anthropogenic Capital		
Manufactured capital	boats of the fleet	roads, buildings, equipment
Human capital	skilled fishers	population health, education distribution
Social capital	regulations on catch	institutions (including rules, norms, rights, culture, networks, etc.)
Knowledge capital	maps of the seabed	Indigenous, scientific, practical, etc.

Source: Clark and Harley 2020.

and that deforestation (the clearest signal of a pre-Contact decline in resources) had more to do with the activities of commensal animals (especially rats) introduced by the progenitors of Rapanui people than it did with any direct actions by its people (beyond their likely inadvertent introduction of rats).

The rock gardens on Rapa Nui are an Indigenous innovation that allowed the people to produce a food surplus on an island with infertile soils and a highly variable environment; that innovation, among others, depended on knowledge capital to create new management practices (a form of manufactured capital). Despite the innovations of Rapanui people, however, Rapa Nui cannot be considered an exemplar of a sustainable society. In 2015, Christopher Stevenson, Sonia Haoa, Thegn Ladefoged, and Oliver Chadwick, all authors of the Rapa Nui chapter, demonstrated that intensive agriculture in lowland sites with relatively fertile soils continued to intensify through Contact and beyond, until Rapa Nui's Polynesian society was destroyed by colonization. Their analysis is strong evidence against a pre-Contact, island-wide collapse. At the same time, they demonstrated that there is evidence for pre-Contact agricultural abandonment in both a nutrient-depleted upland site and in a low-rainfall site, where periodic droughts could have been an external factor contributing to abandonment. If this abandonment was widespread in infertile and unfavorable sites, it implies an island-wide decline in food production associated with loss of natural capital that would have stressed Rapa Nui society at a time when the loss of other resources, especially the loss of forests and attendant resources for canoe building, made the acquisition of marine foods more difficult. These authors suggested that it is more appropriate to consider pre-Contact Rapa Nui as an exemplar of constraint rather than as an exemplar of collapse; in any case, it is not an exemplar of sustainability.

In contrast, Tikopia is perhaps the world's iconic example of a small-scale sustainable society. As the chapter by Patrick Kirch makes clear, most of its productive landscape looks and functions like a complex rain forest, but it is a cultural landscape in which every component of the system is planted and tended and provides people with food and other resources. It is thus perhaps the most striking exemplar of the concept of "ecomimicry" developed by Kawika Winter and colleagues—the idea that the dynamics of Polynesian production systems were based on the dynamics of natural ecosystems, which were modified to yield useful products. Tikopia's extraordinary production system depends on innovations (knowledge capital) that led to the use of new management systems (manufactured capital). Equally important, while agricultural production was and is organized in a way that sustains natural capital—the life-support system of the island—the size of the human population was and is regulated to a level that the resources of the island can support, with some spare capacity to cope with perturbations like damaging storms. In other writing on Tikopia, Kirch has suggested that Tikopia's size—it is the smallest of the islands considered here, only 4.6 square kilometers, less than a 30th the size of Rapa Nui, the next smallest—supports a common polity, expressed in the saying "*Tatou na Tikopia*" (We, the Tikopia). The close societal connection and oneness that this implies may be a strong example of the importance of social capital, where some degree of trust, a culture, and an agreed-upon governance system made even decisions about population control possible.

Along with size, Kirch suggests that soil fertility has been critical to Tikopia's success. Tikopia is a young andesitic volcano, and its soils are not as depleted in nutrients as older volcanic soils are, especially where erosion on the steep slopes brings little-weathered rock into contact with plant roots. In contrast, the other islands considered here support recently active volcanoes, some fertile soils, and some old, nutrient-depleted soils that make sustained agriculture challenging. This contrast is even more striking in comparison to other islands not considered here; Kirch contrasts Tikopia with Mangaia, a Polynesian island with an ancient nutrient-depleted volcanic central core. As Kirch points out, young substrates (a form of natural capital) provide resilience; members of a society based on an island with ancient infertile soils may decide to make a transition to a more sustainable system but be constrained from doing so by a lack of natural capital if their earlier activities destroyed the residual fertility of their soils; a society based on a younger island could have many more options available to it. Natural capital makes sustainability easier once a decision for sustainability is made; other assets, such as social capital, are likely to drive a decision to seek a more sustainable society.

As Kirch also makes clear, the current production system of Tikopia was not the original system; rather, there was a transition from a less to a more sustainable social and production system. As this history demonstrates, the worldview of the Tikopia people did not take them automatically to their remarkable sustainable system. Rather, their close relationship with their social-environmental system motivated them to make a transition to a more sustainable way of living (much as our shared global society needs to do), drawing on all their assets to do so. There is independent evidence based on stable carbon and nitrogen isotopes in commensal (human-associated) rats for this transition on Tikopia; J. A. Swift and colleagues have demonstrated that while most Polynesian islands show a monotonic change in nitrogen isotopes in rats following human occupation, Tikopia initially displayed a decline and then partially recovered during the time its extraordinary agricultural system was implemented.

The pathway taken in Hawai'i was very different from that taken in Tikopia—unsurprisingly, given the enormous differences in the islands. The Hawaiian Archipelago is the second largest of the Polynesian island groups (second to Aotearoa), with 16,698 square kilometers of land. It also gives a home to the one Polynesian society that developed recognizable nations (complex forms of social capital), several of them on the major islands and groups of islands, each with a hereditary kingship, a strong multilevel hierarchy, and the ability to carry out large-scale public works. Over time, the large human populations and large-scale social organizations—human and social capital assets—of Hawai'i facilitated unity within the nations of Hawai'i, probably with a greater top-down organizational component in Hawai'i than in Tikopia. Moreover, the ability to mobilize labor (human capital) for large-scale public works allowed the development of productive systems that would have been difficult or impossible to duplicate in smaller societies, just as it allowed for the development of the armies of conquest that ultimately led to the political unification of the whole Hawaiian Archipelago.

The scale of agricultural innovations in Hawaiian society is remarkable. Polynesian discoverers likely arrived in Hawai'i and Kaua'i, the islands considered in this book, with taro paddies (lo'i kalo), shifting cultivation, and home gardens in their toolkit; aquaculture was widely practiced within the taro paddies. In Hawai'i, large rain-fed field systems with substantial physical infrastructure were developed (as in Kona and Kohala) as an Indigenous invention; so, too, were reef-flat fishponds for marine aquaculture. There is evidence that shortly before European contact, cultivators were beginning to tunnel into incised streams, bringing water and dissolved nutrients to upland fields and again expanding the productive base of society. The creation of these innovations and their implementation in agriculture illustrates the degree to which the Hawaiian society valued and drew on knowledge and manufactured capital assets; although their agricultural systems are not inherently more creative than the cultural forests of Tikopia, the rock gardens of Rapa Nui, or the seasonal food storage of Aotearoa, they are of a form capable of feeding substantially more people than on the other islands. Whereas individual Rapa Nui rock gardens occupied several hundred square meters, several rainfed field systems in Hawai'i occupied tens of millions of square meters; the social and human capital that was needed to support this level of activity had to have been distinctly different, and an understanding of the social capital that facilitated these innovations would enrich our understanding of this Indigenous society, and might suggest paths toward sustainability for global societies.

Was late pre-Contact Hawaiian society sustainable? One argument for its sustainability is the nature of the components of its production system. The classic *ahupua'a* system set out in the Hawai'i chapter and the related larger-scale *moku* system have been described by Kawika Winter and others as an integrated land-division system that could include forests, streams, flooded fields, and fishponds as well as nearshore reefs. Managing all of those areas as an integrated system could be sustainable in a way that a focus on individual components could never be, and integration required that all capital assets be brought to bear. Agricultural production in the rain-fed field systems was maintained for centuries; although flooded fields have been farmed sustainably for many centuries elsewhere (notably, rice fields in East Asia), upland (nonflooded) fields have been more difficult to sustain outside Hawai'i—especially in tropical environments.

An argument against sustainability in pre-Contact Hawaiian society is that there was no Tikopia-like consensus on population in which both cultural and political forces aligned to bring population into balance with production. There is no way to know whether the social capital of the unified islands would have been sufficient to support that development.

What is clear is that Hawai'i is unique among the Polynesian societies discussed here owing to its scale, its ability to mobilize its assets (including labor, creativity, management, technology, and organizational and decision-making approaches) to create new systems that could produce the

food needed to support a complex society over many generations. It may be that seeing nature and the environment as kin,
coupled with genealogical chants that developed relationships
between species from the uplands and the sea, laid a foundation
for seeing the connections between terrestrial and marine
environments—an example of what we might call systems
thinking today.

Given these island examples, we might usefully ask what
the sustainability of past Polynesian societies and their present
expressions could contribute to a current, global transition to
sustainability. Our sense (which can be only a sense, not a firm
conclusion) is that Polynesian societies generally, and pre-Contact
Hawaiian society in particular, have a great deal to teach the world
about sustainability. We see Polynesian societies as dynamic and
innovative places. In some cases people first tried to apply the
production systems of their ancestors. They were able to do so
in some places (where natural capital assets allowed them to do
so), and then—when growth of their population and demand
for yields exceeded the ability of their ancestral systems to provide
for everyone—they mobilized the labor and creativity of their
population (their human and social capital assets) to invent and
to implement a series of new production systems (which
represented new knowledge capital assets and new manufactured
capital assets) that made use of the natural capital assets of
their places. The social-environmental systems that encompassed
both ancestral and locally innovated systems were as sustainable
as the people's considerable ingenuity and capacity for work could
make them (and as sustainable as their natural capital assets allowed); they continued to yield food for many generations
without degrading the resource base that supported them. Pre-
Contact Hawaiian society may be particularly useful as a model
because of its scale and the complexity of its social organization,
which enabled it to mobilize labor and creativity to create new

systems that could produce the food needed to support a complex society.

Overall, we identify four components of a Polynesian worldview that could have encouraged the development of sustainable societies and production systems on Pacific islands:

1. their existence as island societies, of their time and place in a way that most current societies are not
2. the view of plants, animals, and features of the environment as kin, often ancestors
3. a genealogical perspective in which the present generation was viewed as a link in a chain stretching from deep in the past to far in the future
4. a combination of these three components that facilitated innovation at scale and promoted a systems-thinking approach toward problem solving

The first of these is particularly interesting now that the society of the twenty-first century is globalized. Images from space show Earth as a habitable island in the hostile-to-life environment of space, our measurements of the atmosphere show that even our waste products loom large on a global scale, and our observations and models show that our climate everywhere is changing as a consequence of our activities. Since we can now see ourselves as islanders, as Polynesians could, will we be able to build more sustainable societies, as at least some Polynesians did?

Nevertheless, perhaps the most important knowledge we can gain from our review of island societies is that many of our contemporary societies lack the kind of relational understanding of natural systems and environments that enabled the islanders to develop and adapt resource management and food systems across vastly different landscapes. The dominant approaches taken in modern societies show a lack of awareness of the patterns and shifts taking place in the natural systems and heavily discount the value of the future in decision making. This narrow and short-sighted perspective leads some societies to destroy natural systems and, for example, impose industrial agriculture on landscapes rather than adapt to natural systems, adjust them, and shape our societies around them.

Living on a bridge between Indigenous and conventional knowledge systems, we have the ability to bring the best of both worlds to the design, development, and sustainability of the social-environmental systems that support us all. If individuals in modern societies could recognize and cultivate their relationships with natural systems and if we could shape our societies around those relationships, we could follow in the innovative footsteps of our ancestors to live more sustainably on our planet. What our study of islanders' social-environmental systems suggests is that we must act with the foresight of our ancestors and become both the descendants and the ancestors that our human family and our nonhuman world needs us to be.

Glossary of Selected Terms

Islanders have their own terms for the land and the water and their ways of living. Some of those terms are used in the text. This list includes many of them, as well as others that could have been used. Those used in the four island societies considered here are labeled:

H   Hawai'i
M   Māori
RN Rapa Nui
T   Tikopia

All translations, especially brief ones, are incomplete. They may capture one level of what a word means but miss its connotations. Definitions like these will certainly miss the worldview within which the word is used.

ahi   yellowfin tuna
ahu   ceremonial platforms (RN)
ahupua'a   traditional land division, smaller than *moku* (H)
'āina   inhabited land (literally, "that which feeds")
'āina malo'o   rainfed cropland or dryland cultivation (H)
aku   skipjack tuna

akua/atua   gods, elemental deities (H, M)

akule   big-eye scad; mackerel scad

ali'i/ariki   hereditary chiefs (H, M, T)

ali'i nui/ariki nui   paramount chief (H, M)

'āpa'a   the zone of most intensive cultivation of food
   plants (H)

ariki nui   See *ali'i nui/ariki nui*

atua   See *akua/atua*

a'u   marlin

'ea   governance

fono   proclamation (T)

futi   bananas (T)

hala   screwpine (H)

hale/whare   houses (H, M)

hana   work

hapū   clan or subtribe (M)

hau   the winds (M)

hau and *hā*   breath of the gods (wind) and their presence
   (M, H)

he'e   octopus

heiau, marae, ahu   loosely, temples (H, RN)

hikina   arrival

hinengaro   spleen or, expanded, the mind; *finagalo'* on
   Samoa

honua   earth, land without people; Earth (the whole
   globe)

hue   bottle gourd (RN)

hui kū 'ai 'āina   community land groups (H)

huliau   resurgence; period of rapid change (H)

ifi   Tahitian chestnut (T)

'ike   knowledge, or "that which is seen"

'ili   lands managed and used at the family level (H)

imu kai   a fishery technique in which stones are aggregated and piled just offshore (H)

ipu   bottle gourd (H)

iwi   tribe; the bones of an ancestor from whom the tribe descends (M)

kahakai   coastal, nearshore

kahakō/tohutō   macron (H, M)

kahuna/tohunga   high priest (H, M)

kai/tai   ocean, salt water

kalo   taro

kalu'ulu (contraction of *ka ulu 'ulu*)   breadfruit grove

kama'āina   children of the land

kānaka   Native Hawaiian

kānaka maoli/māori/māohi   the original people of this land (H, M, Tahiti/Marquesas)

kānāwai   laws, rules

kānehoalani   sun

kapa/tapa   cloth for clothes and other linen

kapu/tapu   sacred rules, sacredness

karaka   *Corynocarpus laevigatus* (M)

karakia   chant; incantation (M)

kaula   betel-nut palm (T)

kavariki   tropical almond (T)

Kei a te po   in the night (M)

kī/tī   ti; *Cordyline* spp.

kiokio fish   *Chanos chanos* (T)

kīpuka   refuges (literally, "islands of forest surrounded by younger lava flows") (H)

kō   sugarcane (H)

koa   *Acacia koa* trees (H)

koʻa   managed fishing spots; also fishing shrines (H)

koʻi   adzes (H)

konohiki   managers of *ahupuaʻa* (literally, "to invite willingness or ability") (H)

koʻolau   northeasterly trade winds (H)

kopi   *Corynocarpus laevigatus* (T)

kuaiwi   mounds that are the hallmark of intensive dryland agriculture in Hawaiʻi (H)

kuapā   stone-walled fishponds (H)

kukui   candlenut tree

kula   lowland (H)

kumara/ʻuala   sweet potato (M, RN, H)

kumu   teacher

kūpuna/tīpuna   elders; ancestors (H, M)

kūpuna mahiʻai   experienced farmers (H)

lawaiʻa   fishers (H)

limu   seaweed, macroalgae (H)

limu kohu   a red alga (H)

loʻi   paddies or pondfields

loʻi kalo   taro paddies (H)

loko iʻa   fishponds for aquaculture (H)

lokowai   freshwater ponds or pools (H)

Māhele   division of rights to the land in 1848 (H)

mahiʻai   farmers or cultivators (H)

mahinga kai   the practice of food gathering and the place where food is gathered; places for getting food (M)

maiʻa   banana or plantain (H)

makaʻāinana   people of the land, commoners (H)

ma kai   near or toward the sea (H)

makani   wind (H)

malo   traditional clothing (H)

mamaki   a widespread native plant (H)

mami   upas (T)

manava or *manawa* (in Māori)   to explain the idea of having different opinions (M)

manavai   rock-walled gardens (RN)

manawa   heart (M)

manini   convict tang (H)

masi pits   pits for storing fermented food (T)

matafonua   head or face of the land; senior half of a division of territory (M)

mātauranga Māori   Māori knowledge systems, epistemology (M)

ma uka   in the uplands; upslope; toward the mountains (H)

mauna/maunga   mountain (H, M)

mauri   the essence of an ancestral spirit; though generally seen as the "life essence of the ancestor," it may be better to understand it as the presence of an ancestral spirit (M)

mei   breadfruit (T)

mele ko'i honua   genealogical cosmologies (H)

moa   large flightless birds (M)

moai   statues (RN)

moku   large land divisions that contain multiple *ahupua'a* (H)

mokupuni   island-scale land division comprising multiple *moku* (H)

mo'olelo, ka'ao   oral histories (H)

nenue   Hawaiian chub (H)

ngākau   intestines; seat of affection, of mental pain, of thought (M)

ngau marama   "biting the moon," the approach of Venus to the moon (M)

niu   coconut palm (H, T)
noni   *Morinda citrifolia*, Indian mulberry (H)

'ohana/whānau   families (H, M)
'ohi   gathering (H)
'o'io   bonefish (H)
'ōiwi   Indigenous (Native) Hawaiian (H)
'okina   glottal stop (H)
'ōpelu   mackerel scad (H)
ota   sago palm (T)

pā   fortified site or village (M)
pa'akai   salt (H)
pae 'āina   archipelago
pae 'āina o Hawai'i   Hawaiian archipelago (H)
pāhoehoe   smooth and ropy-textured (lava flow) (H)
Pakeha   White people, Europeans (M)
pākukui   swidden or shifting cultivation with a managed
    fallow system (H)
pālena   boundaries of a place (H)
pāpa'i   crab (H)
poho   depressions
pounamu   New Zealand greenstone, jade (M)
pu-kanohi   lagoons along estuaries (M)
pulaka   giant swamp taro (T)
pulaka vao   cultivar of *pulaka* (T)
punawai   springs (H)
'pūnui-o-toka   southerly wind (M)

Rangatira   chief, leader (M)
ruahine   woman elder, who is no longer subject to the restric-
    tions of *tapu;* also known as the *pa-whaka-wairua* (M)
ruru   morepork owl (M)

taiao   environment

tāmaki   an omen or sign where an individual's muscles twitch or have convulsive movements (M)

tapu   See *kapu/tapu*

taro   taro (M, RN, T)

Te Ara Tapu   pathway for spirits across Aotearoa (M)

Te Hiku o te Ika ā Maui, or *muriwhenua*   "the tail of Maui's fish," the north of the North Island of New Zealand (M)

Te Ika ā Maui   "Maui's fish," the North Island of New Zealand (M)

tēina   junior (M)

Te Upoko ō te Ika ā Maui   "the head of Maui's fish," at Cook Strait (M)

Te Wai Pounamu   "the land of jade," the South Island of New Zealand (M)

Te Waka ō Māui   the canoe of Maui; the South Island of New Zealand (M)

tī   See *kī/tī*

tīpuna   See *kūpuna/tīpuna*

tohu   signs and omens, voices of our ancestors (M)

tohunga   See *kahuna/tohunga*

tuākana   senior (M)

'uala   See *kumara/'uala*

'uhi   yam

'ulu   breadfruit (H)

uluhiku   "tail of the fish," junior half of a division of territory (M); also called *ulifonua*

ulu lā'au   arboriculture, agroforestry (H)

vere   cut nut (T)

vi   vi apple (T)

voia   sea almond (T)

wa'a/waka   canoe (H, M)

wahi-tapu   sacred land or a holy site (M)

wai   fresh water (H)

wairua   spirit or soul; spirit that exists within the person (M)

waiwai   goods, property, assets, valuables, value, worth, wealth, importance, benefit, estate, use (H)

waka   See *wa'a/waka*

waka taua   war canoe (M)

wakawaka   parcels of land or other resources (M)

wana   sea urchin (H)

wao akua   the unaltered forest that was considered the realm of the gods (H)

wauke   paper mulberry (H, RN)

wehena   opening (H)

weka   woodhen (M)

whakapapa   genealogies (M)

whānau   See *ohana/whānau*

whare   See *hale/whare*

whare pūrākau   sacred schools of learning (M)

whare wānanga or *whare pūrākau*   traditional buildings where sacred knowledge was passed on from tribal elders to the next generation (M)

Selected References and Suggestions for Further Reading

Introduction

Darwin, C. *The Voyage of the Beagle.* New York: F. C. Collier and Son, 1909.

Gavrilets, S., and J. B. Losos. "Adaptive Radiation: Contrasting Theory with Data." *Science* 323 (2009): 732–737.

Kirch, P. V. "Three Islands and an Archipelago: Reciprocal Interactions between Humans and Island Ecosystems in Polynesia." *Earth and Environmental Science Transactions of the Royal Society of Edinburgh* 98 (2007): 85–99.

Chapter 1. Who Are the Polynesians and What Is Polynesia?

Cook, J. *A Voyage Towards the South Pole and Round the World.* Vol. 1. 1777. Republished. Frankfurt am Main, Germany: Outlook-Verlag, 2018.

Chapter 2. Polynesian Islands as Model Social-Environmental Systems

Fitzpatrick, S. M., and J. M. Erlandson. "Island Archaeology, Model Systems, the Anthropocene, and How the Past Informs the Future." *Journal of Island and Coastal Archaeology* 13 (2018): 283–299, https://doi.org/10.1080/15564894.2018.1447051.

Kirch, P. V. "Hawaii as a Model System for Human Ecodynamics." *American Anthropologist* 109 (2007): 8–26.

Kirch, P. V. "Microcosmic Histories: Island Perspectives on 'Global' Change." *American Anthropologist* 99 (1997): 30–42.

Leppard, T. P., R. J. DiNapoli, J. F. Cherry, K. Douglass, J. M. Erlandson, T. L. Hunt, P. V. Kirch, C. P. Lipo, S. O'Connor, S. E. Pilaar Birch, T. C. Rick, T. M. Rieth, and J. A. Swift. "The Premise and Potential of Model-Based Approaches to Island Archaeology: A Response to Terrell." *Journal of Island and Coastal Archaeology* (2021), https://doi.org/10.1080/15564894.2021.190 4463.

Terrell, J. E. "Metaphor and Theory in Island Archaeology." *Journal of Island and Coastal Archaeology* (2020), https://doi.org/10.1080/15564894.2020.18 30892.

Vitousek, P. M. *Nutrient Cycling and Limitation: Hawai'i as a Model System.* Princeton, NJ: Princeton University Press, 2004.

Vitousek, P. M. "Oceanic Islands as Model Systems for Ecological Studies." *Journal of Biogeography* 29 (2002): 573–582.

Chapter 3. Hawai'i

Abbott, I. A. *Lā'au Hawai'i: Traditional Hawaiian Uses of Plants.* Honolulu: Bishop Museum Press, 1992.

Beamer, K. *No Mākou ka Mana: Liberating the Nation.* Honolulu: Kamehameha Publishing, 2014.

Cachola-Abad, C. K. *The Evolution of Hawaiian Socio-political Complexity: An Analysis of Hawaiian Oral Traditions.* Honolulu: University of Hawai'i, 2000.

Desha, S. L. *Kamehameha and His Warrior Kekūhaupi'o.* Honolulu: Kamehameha Publishing, 2000.

Edith Kanaka'ole Foundation. *Kanawai Honuamea.* Hilo, HI: Edith Kanaka'ole Foundation, 2013.

Freidlander, A., K. Poepoe, K. Poepoe, K. Helm, et al. "Application of Hawaiian Traditions to Community-Based Fishery Management." *Proceedings 9th International Coral Reef Symposium* 2 (2000): 813–818.

Handy, E. S., E. G. Handy, and M. K. Pukui. *Native Planters in Old Hawaii: Their Life, Lore, and Environment.* Vol. 233. Honolulu: Bishop Museum, 1972.

Handy, E. S. C., and M. K. Pukui. *Polynesian Family System in Ka'ū Hawaii.* Rutland, VT: Tuttle Publishing, 2012.

Hommon, R. J. *The Ancient Hawaiian State: Origins of a Political Society.* Oxford: Oxford University Press, 2013.

Ho'oulumāhiehie. "Ka Moolelo o Hiiakaikapoliopele." *Ka Nai Aupuni,* January 22, 1906. Translated in M. P. Nogelmeier, *Ka Moolelo o Hiiakaikapoliopele* (Honolulu: University of Hawai'i Press, 2013).

Kamakau, S. M. *Ruling Chiefs of Hawai'i.* Honolulu: Kamehameha Schools Press, 1961.

Kanahele, P. K., K. Kealiikanakaoleohaililani, H. Kanahele-Mossman, K. Nuʻuhiwa, et al. *Kīhoʻihoʻi Kānāwai: Restoring Kānāwai for Island Stewardship.* Honolulu: Edith Kanakaʻole Foundation, 2016.

Kealiikanakaoleohaililani, K., N. Kurashima, K. S. Francisco, C. P. Giardina, et al. "Ritual + Sustainability Science? A Portal into the Science of Aloha." *Sustainability* 10 (2018): 3478.

Kirch, P. V. *Feathered Gods and Fishhooks: An Introduction to Hawaiian Archaeology and Prehistory.* Honolulu: University of Hawaiʻi Press, 1985.

Kirch, P. V., and K. S. Zimmerer. *Roots of Conflict.* Santa Fe, NM: School for Advanced Research, 2011.

Kurashima, N., J. Jeremiah, A. N. Whitehead, J. Tulchin, et al. " ʻĀina Kaumaha: The Maintenance of Ancestral Principles for 21st Century Indigenous Resource Management." *Sustainability* 10 (2018): 3975, https://doi.org/10.3390/su10113975.

Lincoln, N. K., J. Rossen, P. M. Vitousek, J. Kahoonei, et al. "Restoration of ʻĀina Maloʻo on Hawaiʻi Island: Expanding Biocultural Relationships." *Sustainability* 10 (2018): 3985.

Lincoln, N. K., and P. M. Vitousek. "Indigenous Polynesian Agriculture in Hawaiʻi." In *Oxford Research Encyclopedia of Environmental Science.* Oxford: Oxford University Press, 2017.

MacKenzie, M. K., S. K. Serrano, D. K. Sproat, A. K. Obrey, and A. K. Poai, eds. *Native Hawaiian Law: A Treatise.* Honolulu: Kamehameha Publishing, 2015.

Malo, D. *Ka Moolelo Hawaii / Hawaiian Antiquities.* Honolulu: Bishop Museum, 1981.

Silva, N. K. *The Power of the Steel-Tipped Pen: Reconstructing Native Hawaiian Intellectual History.* Durham, NC: Duke University Press, 2017.

Vaughan, M. B. *Kaiaulu: Gathering Tides.* Corvallis: Oregon State University Press, 2018.

Winter, K. B. "*Kalo* (Hawaiian Taro, *Colocasia esculenta* (L.) Schott) Varieties: An Assessment of Nomenclatural Synonymy and Biodiversity." *Ethnobotany Research and Applications* 10 (2012): 423–447.

Winter, K. B., K. Beamer, M. B. Vaughan, A. M. Friedlander, et al. "The *Moku* System: Managing Biocultural Resources for Abundance within Social-Ecological Regions in Hawaiʻi." *Sustainability* 10 (2018): 3554, https://doi.org/10.3390/su10103554.

Winter, K. B., M. B. Vaughn, N. Kurashima, L. Wann, E. Cadiz, and H. K. Springer. "Novel Approaches to Collaborative Management of Indigenous and Community Conserved Areas in Hawaiʻi." *Ecology and Society* (2022).

Winter, K. B., M. Vaughn, N. Kurashima, C. Giardina, et al. "Empowering Indigenous Agency through Community-Driven Collaborative Management to Achieve Effective Conservation: Hawai'i as an Example." *Pacific Conservation Biology* 27 (2021): 337–344, https://doi.org/10.1071/PC20009.

Chapter 4. Rapa Nui (Easter Island) Rock Gardens

Anda, M., J. Shamshuddin, C. I. Fauziah, S. R. S. Omar. "Dissolution of Ground Basalt and Its Effect on Oxisol Chemical Properties and Cocoa Growth." *Soil Science* 174 (2009): 264–271.

Baer, A., T. N. Ladefoged, C. M. Stevenson, and S. Haoa. "The Surface Rock Gardens of Prehistoric Rapa Nui." *Rapa Nui Journal* 22 (2008): 102–109.

Cañellas-Boltà, N., V. Rull, A. Sàez, O. Margalef, et al. "Vegetation Changes and Human Settlement of Easter Island during the Last Millennia: A Multiproxy Study of the Lake Raraku Sediments." *Quaternary Science Reviews* 72 (2013): 36–48.

Flenley, J., and P. Bahn. *The Enigmas of Easter Island: Island on the Edge.* New York: Oxford University Press, 2002.

Fyfe, W. S., O. H. Leonardos, and S. H. Theodoro. "Sustainable Farming with Native Rocks: The Transition without Revolution." *Annals of the Brazilian Academy of Sciences* 78 (2006): 715–720.

Hensel, J. *Bread from Stones: A New and Rational System of Land Fertilization and Physical Regeneration.* Philadelphia, PA: A. J. Tafel, 1894.

Horrocks, M., and J. A. Wozniak. "Plant Microfossil Analysis Reveals Disturbed Forest and a Mixed-Crop Dryland Production System at Te Niu, Easter Island." *Journal of Archaeological Science* 35 (2008): 126–142.

Hunt, T. L., and C. P. Lipo. *The Statues That Walked: Unraveling the Mystery of Easter Island.* New York: Free Press, 2011.

Ladefoged, T. N., A. Flaws, and C. M. Stevenson. "The Distribution of Rock Gardens on Rapa Nui (Easter Island) as Determined from Satellite Imagery." *Journal of Archaeological Science* 40 (2013): 1203–1212.

Ladefoged, T. N., C. M. Stevenson, S. Haoa, M. Mulrooney, et al. "Soil Nutrient Analysis of Rapa Nui Gardening." *Archaeology in Oceania* 45 (2010): 80–85.

Ladefoged, T. N., C. M. Stevenson, P. M. Vitousek, and O. A. Chadwick. "Soil Nutrient Depletion and the Collapse of Rapa Nui Society." *Rapa Nui Journal* 19 (2005): 100–105.

Lopes, O. M. M., E. N. V. M. Carrilho, and M. L. R. C. Lopes-Assad. "Effect of Rock Powder and Vinasse on Two Types of Soils." *Revista Brasileira de Ciência do Solo* 38 (2014): 1547–1557.

Louwagie, G., C. M. Stevenson, and R. Langohr. "The Impact of Moderate to Marginal Land Suitability on Prehistoric Agricultural Production and Models of Adaptive Strategies for Easter Island (Rapa Nui, Chile)." *Journal of Anthropological Archaeology* 25 (2006): 290–317.

Mann, D., J. Edwards, J. Chase, W. Beck, et al. "Drought, Vegetation Change, and Human History on Rapa Nui (Isla de Pascua, Easter Island)." *Quaternary Research* 69 (2008): 16–28.

Mieth, A., and H. R. Bork. "Diminution and Degradation of Environmental Resources by Prehistory Land Use on Poike Peninsula, Easter Island (Rapa Nui)." *Rapa Nui Journal* 17 (2003): 34–41.

Mieth, A., and H. R. Bork. "History, Origin and Extent of Soil Erosion on Easter Island (Rapa Nui)." *Catena* 63 (2005): 244–260.

Mulrooney, M. A. "An Island-Wide Assessment of the Chronology of Settlement and Land Use on Rapa Nui (Easter Island) Based on Radiocarbon Data." *Journal of Archaeological Science* 40 (2013): 4377–4399.

Mulrooney, M. A., T. N. Ladefoged, C. M. Stevenson, and S. Haoa. "Empirical Assessment of a Pre-European Societal Collapse on Rapa Nui (Easter Island)." In P. Wallin and H. Martinsson-Wallin, eds., *The Gotland Papers: Selected Papers from the VII International Conference on Easter Island and the Pacific: Migration, Identity, and Cultural Heritage*, 141–154. Gotland, Sweden: Gotland University, 2010.

Nunes, J. M. G., R. M. Kautzmann, and C. Oliveria. "Evaluation of the Natural Fertilizing Potential of Basalt Dust Wastes from the Mining District of Nova Prata (Brazil)." *Journal of Cleaner Production* 84 (2014): 649–656.

Puleston, C. O., T. N. Ladefoged, S. Haoa, O. A. Chadwick, et al. "Rain, Sun, Soil, and Sweat: A Consideration of Population Limits on Rapa Nui (Easter Island) before European Contact." *Frontiers in Ecology and Evolution* 5 (2017): 1–14.

Rainbird, P. "A Message for Our Future? The Rapa Nui (Easter Island) Eco-disaster and Pacific Island Environments." *World Archaeology* 33 (2002): 436–451.

Ramos, C. G., A. G. de Mello, and R. M. Kautzmann. "A Preliminary Study of Acid Volcanic Rocks for Stonemeal Application." *Environmental Nanotechnology, Monitoring & Management* 1–2 (2014): 30–35.

Routledge, K. *The Mystery of Easter Island*. London: Hazell, Watson, and Viney, 1919.

Rull, V., N. Cañellas-Boltà, O. Margalef, S. Pla-Rabes, et al. "Three Millennia of Climatic, Ecological and Cultural Change on Easter Island: An Integrative Overview." *Frontiers in Ecology and Evolution* 4 (2016): 29, https://doi.org/10.3389/fevo.2016.00029.

Rull, V., N. Cañellas-Boltà, A. Sáez, O. Margalef, et al. "Challenging Easter Island's Collapse: The Need for Interdisciplinary Synergies." *Frontiers in Ecology and Evolution* 2 (2013): 56, https://doi.org/10.3389/fevo.2013.00003.

Sherwood, S. C., J. A. V. Tilburg, C. R. Barrier, and M. Horrocks. "New Excavations in Easter Island's Statue Quarry: Soil Fertility, Site Formation and Chronology." *Journal of Archaeological Science* 111 (2019), https://doi.org/10.1016/j.jas.2019.104994.

Steadman, D. W., C. Vargas, and F. Cristino. "Stratigraphy, Chronology, and Cultural Context of an Early Faunal Assemblage from Easter Island." *Asian Perspectives* 33 (1994): 79–96.

Stevenson, C. M., and S. Haoa Cardinali. *Prehistoric Rapa Nui: Landscape and Settlement Archaeology at Hanga Ho'onu.* Los Osos, CA: Easter Island Foundation, 2008.

Stevenson, C. M., T. L. Jackson, A. Mieth, H. R. Bork, et al. "Prehistoric and Early Historic Agriculture at Maunga Orito, Easter Island (Rapa Nui), Chile." *Antiquity* 80 (2006): 919–936.

Stevenson, C. M., C. Puleston, P. M. Vitousek, O. A. Chadwick, et al. "Variation in Rapa Nui (Easter Island) Land Use Indicates Production and Population Peaks prior to European Contact." *Proceedings of the National Academy of Sciences* 112 (2015): 1025–1030.

Stevenson, C. M., J. Wozniak, and S. Haoa. "Prehistoric Agricultural Production on Easter Island (Rapa Nui), Chile." *Antiquity* 73 (1999): 801–812.

Vargas, P., C. Cristino, and R. Izaurieta. *1000 Años en Rapa Nui: Arqueología del asentamiento.* Santiago, Chile: Editorial Universitaria, 2006.

Vitousek, P. M., O. A. Chadwick, S. C. Hotchkiss, T. N. Ladefoged, and C. M. Stevenson. "Farming the Rock: A Biogeochemical Perspective on Intensive Agriculture in Polynesia." *Journal of Pacific Archaeology* 5 (2014): 51–61.

Wilmshurst, J. M., T. L. Hunt, C. P. Lipo, and A. J. Anderson. "High-Precision Radiocarbon Dating Shows Recent and Rapid Initial Human Colonization of East Polynesia." *Proceedings of the National Academy of Sciences* 108 (2011): 1815–1820.

Wozniak, J. A. *Exploring Landscapes on Easter Island (Rapanui) with Geoarchaeological Studies: Settlement, Subsistence, and Environmental Changes.* PhD dissertation, University of Oregon, 2003.

Wozniak, J. A. "Prehistoric Horticultural Practices on Easter Island: Lithic Mulched Gardens and Field Systems." *Rapa Nui Journal* 13 (1999): 95–99.

Wozniak, J. A. "Subsistence Strategies on Rapa Nui (Easter Island): Prehistoric Gardening Practices on Rapa Nui and How They Relate to Current Farming Practices." In S. Haoa, K. B. Ingersoll, D. W. Ingersoll Jr., and C. M. Stevenson, eds., *Cultural and Environmental Change on Rapa Nui,* 87–112. London: Routledge, 2018.

Chapter 5. Tikopia

Borrie, W. D., R. Firth, and J. Spillius. "The Population of Tikopia, 1929 and 1952." *Population Studies* 3 (1957): 229–252.

Dillon, P. *Narrative and Successful Result of a Voyage in the South Seas Performed by Order of the Government of British India, to Ascertain the Actual Fate of La Pérouse's Expedition Interspersed with Accounts of the Religion, Manners, Customs and Cannibal Practices of the South Sea Islanders.* Volume II. London: Hurst, Chance, 1929.

Firth, R. *Social Change in Tikopia.* New York: MacMillan, 1959.

Firth, R. *We, the Tikopia.* London: George Allen and Unwin, 1936.

Firth, R. *The Work of the Gods in Tikopia.* 2nd ed. London: Athlone, 1967.

Kirch, P. V. *The Wet and the Dry: Irrigation and Agricultural Intensification in Polynesia.* Chicago: University of Chicago Press, 1994.

Kirch, P. V., and D. E. Yen. *Tikopia: The Prehistory and Ecology of a Polynesian Outlier.* Bishop Museum Bulletin 238. Honolulu: Bishop Museum, 1982.

Chapter 6. Mahinga kai nō Tonganui (New Zealand)

Anderson, A. "Changing Perspectives upon Māori Colonisation Voyaging." *Journal of the Royal Society of New Zealand* 47 (2017): 222–231.

Anderson, A. "Islands from the South: An Oceanic Perspective on Island Colonisation." In N. Phoca-Cosmetatou, ed., *The First Mediterranean Islanders: Initial Occupation and Survival Strategies,* 157–172. Monograph 74. Oxford: University of Oxford School of Archaeology, 2011.

Anderson, A. "Kin and Border: Traditional Land Boundaries in East Polynesia and New Zealand with Particular Reference to the Northern Boundary of Ngai Tahu." Unpublished evidence to Waitangi Tribunal, Wellington, NZ. Department of Justice, 2003.

Anderson, A. "The Making of the Māori Middle Ages: J. D. Stout Lecture." *Journal of New Zealand Studies* 23 (2016): 2–11.

Anderson, A. "Monumentality and Ritual Behaviour in South Polynesia." In H. Martinsson-Wallin and T. Thomas, eds., *Monuments and People in the Pacific,* 273–296. Uppsala, Sweden: Uppsala University Press, 2014.

Anderson, A. "Using Numbers from Somewhere Else: Comment on Chapple's "New Zealand Numbers from Nearly Nowhere: 80,000 to 100,000 Maori circa 1769." *New Zealand Journal of History* 51 (2017): 122–125.

Anderson, A. *The Welcome of Strangers: An Ethnohistory of Southern Maori, AD 1650–1850.* Dunedin, NZ: Otago University Press, 1998.

Anderson, A., J. Binney, and A. Harris. *Tangata Whenua: An Illustrated History.* Wellington, NZ: Bridget Williams Books, 2014.

Anderson, A., and F. Petchey. "The Transfer of Kumara (*Ipomoea batatas*) from East to South Polynesia and Its Dispersal in New Zealand." *Journal of the Polynesian Society* 129 (2020): 351–382.

Anderson, A., and I. Smith. "Shag Mouth as an Early Maori Village." In A. Anderson, B. Allingham, and I. Smith, eds., *Shag River Mouth: The Archaeology of an Early Southern Maori Village,* 276–291. Canberra: Australian National University, 1996.

Barber, I. "Crops on the Border: The Growth of Archaeological Knowledge of Polynesian Cultivation in New Zealand." In L. Furey and S. Holdaway, eds., *Change through Time: 50 Years of New Zealand Archaeology,* 169–192. Auckland: New Zealand Archaeological Association, 2004.

Barber, I. "Diffusion or Innovation? Explaining Extensive Lithic Cultivation Fields on the Southern Polynesian Margins." *World Archaeology* 42 (2010): 75–90.

Barber, I. "Molluscan Mulching at the Margins: Investigating the Development of South Island Maori Variation on Polynesian Hard Mulch Agronomy." *Archaeology in Oceania* 48 (2013): 40–52.

Bassett, K. N., W. G. Hamish, D. C. Nobes, and C. Jacomb. "Gardening at the Edge: Documenting the Limits of Tropical Polynesian Kumara Horticulture in Southern New Zealand." *Geoarchaeology* 19 (2004): 185–218.

Belich, J. *The New Zealand Wars and the Victorian Interpretation of Racial Conflict.* Auckland, NZ: Auckland University Press, 2015.

Brown, A. A., and E. R. Crema. "Māori Population Growth in Pre-contact New Zealand: Regional Population Dynamics Inferred from Summed Probability Distributions of Radiocarbon Dates." *Journal of Island and Coastal Archaeology* (2019). https://doi.org/10.1080/15564894.2019.1605429.

Campbell, M. *Settlement and Landscape in Late Prehistoric Rarotonga, Southern Cook Islands.* PhD thesis, University of Sydney, 2001.

Challis, A. J. *Ka Pakihi Whakatekateka o Waitaha: The Archaeology of Canterbury in Maori Times.* Science and Research Series no. 89. Wellington, NZ: Department of Conservation, 1995.

Challis, A. J. "The Nelson-Marlborough Region: An Archaeological Synthesis." *New Zealand Journal of Archaeology* 13 (1991): 101–142.

Chapple, S. "New Zealand Numbers from Nearly Nowhere: 80,000 to 100,000 Maori circa 1769." *New Zealand Journal of History* 51 (2017): 104–121.

Fagan, B. *The Little Ice Age: How Climate Made History, 1300–1850.* New York: Basic Books, 2000.

Furey, L. *Maori Gardening: An Archaeological Perspective.* Science and Technical Publishing. Wellington, NZ: Department of Conservation, 2006.

Goldman, I. *Ancient Polynesian Society.* Chicago: University of Chicago Press, 1970.

Keegan, W. F. "Modelling Dispersal in the Prehistoric West Indies." *World Archaeology* 26 (1995): 400–420.

Kirch, P. V., and J.-L. Rallu, eds. *The Growth and Collapse of Pacific Island Societies: Archaeological and Demographic Perspectives.* Honolulu: University of Hawaii Press, 2007.

Latham, A. D. M., M. C. Latham, J. M. Wilmshurst, D. M. Forsyth, et al. "A Refined Model of Body Mass and Population Density in Flightless Birds Reconciles Extreme Bimodal Population Estimates for Extinct Moa." *Ecography* 42 (2019): 1–12.

Leach, B. F., A. J. Anderson, D. G. Sutton, R. Bird, et al. "The Origin of Prehistoric Obsidian Artefacts from the Chathams and Kermadec Islands." *New Zealand Journal of Archaeology* 8 (1986): 143–170.

Lorrey, A., P. Williams, J. Salinger, T. Martin, et al. "Speleothem Stable Isotope Records Interpreted with a Multi-proxy Framework and Implications for New Zealand Palaeoclimate Reconstruction." *Quaternary International* 187 (2008): 52–75.

McFadgen, B. *Archaeology of the Wellington Conservancy: Kapiti-Horowhenua. A Prehistoric and Palaeoenvironmental Study.* Wellington, NZ: Department of Conservation, 1997.

McFadgen, B. *Archaeology of the Wellington Conservancy: Wairarapa.* Wellington, NZ: Department of Conservation, 2003.

McWethy, D. B., C. Whitlock, J. M. Wilmshurst, M. S. McGlone, et al. "Rapid Landscape Transformation in South Island, New Zealand, Following Initial Polynesian Settlement." *Proceedings of the National Academy of Sciences USA* 107 (2010): 21343–21348.

Newnham, R., D. J. Lowe, M. Gehrels, and P. Augustinus. "Two-Step Human-Environmental Impact History for Northern New Zealand Linked to Late-Holocene Climate Change." *The Holocene* 28 (2018): 1093–1106.

Penny, D., R. P. Murray-MacIntosh, and G. L. Harrison. "Estimating the Number of Females in the Founding Population of New Zealand: Analysis of mtDNA Variation." *Journal of the Polynesian Society* 111 (2002): 207–221.

Prebble, M., A. J. Anderson, P. Augustinus, J. Emmitt, et al. "Early Tropical Crop Production in Marginal Subtropical and Temperate Polynesia." *Proceedings of the National Academy of Sciences* 116 (2019): 8824–8833.

Sahlins, M. *Historical Ethnography.* Vol. 1 of *Anahulu: The Anthropology of History in the Kingdom of Hawaii,* ed. P. V. Kirch and M. Sahlins. Chicago: University of Chicago Press, 1992.

Smith, N. *Native Custom and Law Affecting the Land.* Wellington, NZ: Maori Purposes Fund Board, 1942, p. 63

Tau, T. M., and A. Anderson. *Ngai Tahu: A Migration History.* Wellington, NZ: Bridget Williams Books, 2008.

Thomson, W. J. *Te Pito o te Henua, or Easter Island.* From US National Museum, annual report, 1889. Washington, DC, 1891.

Weisler, M., and P. V. Kirch. "The Structure of Settlement Space in a Polynesian Chiefdom: Kawela, Molokai, Hawaiian Islands." *New Zealand Journal
of Archaeology* 7 (1985): 129–158.

White, P., C. Reepmeyer, and G. Clark. "A Norfolk Island Basalt Adze from
New South Wales." *Australian Archaeology* 79 (2014): 131–136.

Whyte, A. L., S. J. Marshall, and G. K. Chambers. "Evolution in Polynesia."
Human Biology 77 (2005): 157–177.

Williams, P. W., D. N. T. King, J.-X. Zhao, and K. D. Collerson. "Speleothem
Master Chronologies: Combined Holocene 18O and 13C Records from the
North Island of New Zealand and Their Paleoenvironmental Interpreta-
tion." *The Holocene* 14 (2004): 194–208.

Chapter 7. The Hidden *Pā* of Knowledge and the Mind of Māori

Armstrong, K. *The Great Transformation: The World in the Time of Buddha,
Socrates, Confucius and Jeremiah.* London: Atlantic Books, 2007.

Armstrong, K. *A History of Jerusalem: One City, Three Faiths.* Glasgow, Scot-
land: William Collins, 2005.

Beattie, H. *Maori Lore of Lake, Alp and Fiord: Folk Lore, Fairy Tales, Traditions
and Place-Names of the Scenic Wonderland of the South Island.* Dunedin, NZ:
Otago Daily Times and Witness Newspapers Company, 1945. Reprint, 2014.

Best, E. *Māori Forest Lore: Being Some Account of Native Forest Lore and
Woodcraft, as Also of Many Myths, Rites, Customs and Superstitions Connected with the Flora and Fauna of the Tuhoe Or Ure-wera District.* Wellington, NZ: Government Printer, 2010.

Best, E. *Maori Religion and Mythology.* Wellington, NZ: P. D. Hasselberg,
Government Printer, 1982.

Best, E. *Maori Religion and Mythology.* Part II. Wellington, NZ: P. D. Hasselberg,
Government Printer, 1982.

Best, E. "Spiritual Concepts of the Maori. Part II." *Journal of the Polynesian
Society* 10 (1901): 1–20.

Eliade, M. *The Sacred and the Profane: The Nature of Religion.* No. 144. New
York: Houghton Mifflin Harcourt, 1959.

Hanson, F., and L. Hanson, *Counterpoint in Māori Culture.* London: Routledge
and Kegan Paul, 1983.

Hape, T. Whakapapa Ms Vol. 1, Rima Te Aotukia Bell Archives. Private collection. There are a number of tribal variations to this chant.

McNab, R. *Murihiku: A History of the South Island of New Zealand and the
Islands Adjacent and Lying to the South, from 1642 to 1835.* Cambridge:
Cambridge University Press, 2011.

McRae, J. *Maori Oral Tradition: He Kōrero nō te Ao Tawhito.* Auckland, NZ: Auckland University Press, 2017. The bracketed inserts in the quotation are McRae's.

Ngata, A. T., and P. Te Hurinui Jones. *Ngā Mōteatea.* Parts I and II. Wellington, NZ: The Polynesian Society, 1961, pp. 398–399.

Ngata, A. T., and P. Te Hurinui Jones. *Ngā Mōteatea: The Songs.* Parts One and Two. Auckland, NZ: Auckland University Press, 2004.

Nihoniho, T. *Narrative of the Fighting on the East Coast (Nga Pakanga ki Te Tai Rawhiti).* Wellington, NZ: John Mackay, Government Printer, 1913.

Salmond, A. "The Study of Traditional Maori Society: The State of the Art." *Journal of the Polynesian Society* 92 (1983): 309–331.

Schama, S. *Landscape and Memory.* New York: A. A. Knopf, 1995.

Smith, A. *Taranaki Waiata Tangi and Feelings for Place.* PhD thesis, Lincoln University, 2001.

Rawiri Te Maire Map. Taiaroa ms, #171, p. 157, Taiaroa Map, Between the Rapatu Flat and Lake Hawea. 1880. Also see Taiaroa Map where Te Marara is spelt Maramarua. The sequence of names from the 1880 manuscript runs from Aroraki to Mata Pou, Te Whare Manu, Tiori Patea, Awarua, Te Whiti o Te Wahine, O kopiri, Maramarua, Waitotyo, Pokeka-wera Waitoto, Pokeke-wera, Waitaha, all of which runs into the Te Awawa Makarara.

Te Rangihiroa, *The Coming of the Maori.* Wellington, NZ: Maori Purposes Fund Board, 1949.

Tregear, E. *Maori-Polynesian Comparative Dictionary.* Wellington, NZ: Lyon and Blair, 1891.

Van Bellekom, M., and R. Harlow, eds. *Te Waiatatanga mai o te Atua: South Island Traditions Recorded by Matiaha Tiramorehu.* Christchurch, NZ: Department of Maori, University of Canterbury, 1987.

White, J. *Ancient History of the Maori.* Vol. 1. Wellington, NZ: Government Printer, 1887).

White, J. *Miscellaneous Manuscripts Relating to His Ancient History of the Maori.* Ms Papers 1187–1202. Wellington, NZ: Alexander Turnbull Library, 1887.

Worrell, W. P., ed. *Sir Joseph Banks in New Zealand.* Wellington, NZ: A. H. and A. W. Reed, 1958.

Chapter 8. Similarities and Differences in Island Social-Environmental Systems

Kirch, P. V. "Microcosmic Histories: Island Perspectives on 'Global' Change." *American Anthropologist* 99 (1997): 30–42.

Leppard, T. P. "Rehearsing the Anthropocene in Microcosm: The Palaeoenvironmental Impacts of the Pacific Rat (*Rattus exulans*) and Other

Non-human Species during Island Neolithization." In S. E. P. Birch, ed., *Multispecies Archaeology,* 47–64. London: Routledge, 2018.

Winter, K. B. "*Kalo* (Hawaiian Taro, *Colocasia esculenta* (L.) Schott) Varieties: An Assessment of Nomenclatural Synonymy and Biodiversity." *Ethnobotany Research and Applications* 10 (2012): 423–447.

Winter, K. B., N. K. Lincoln, and F. Berkes. "The Social/Ecological Keystone Concept: A Quantifiable Metaphor for Understanding the Structure, Function, and Resilience of a Biocultural System." *Sustainability* 10 (2018), https://doi.org/10.3390/su10093294.

Chapter 9. Sustainability in Polynesian Island Societies

Clark, W. C., and A. G. Harley. "Sustainability Science: Toward a Synthesis." *Annual Reviews of Environment and Resources* 45 (2020): 331–386.

DasGupta, P. S. "Measuring the Wealth of Nations." *Annual Reviews of Resource Economics* 6 (2014): 17–31.

Matson, P. A., W. C. Clark, and K. Anderson. *Pursuing Sustainability: A Guide to the Science and Practice.* Princeton, NJ: Princeton University Press, 2016.

Sterling, E. J., C. Filardi, A. Toomey, A. Sigouin, et al. "Biocultural Approaches to Well-Being and Sustainability Indicators across Scales." *Nature Ecology and Evolution* 1 (2017): 1798–1806, https://doi.org/10.1038/s41559-017-0349-6.

Swift, J. A., P. V. Kirch, J. Ilgner, S. Brown, M. Lucas, S. Marzo, and P. Roberts. "Stable Isotopic Evidence for Nutrient Rejuvenation and Long-Term Resilience on Tikopia Island (Southeast Solomon Islands)." *Sustainability* 13 (2021): 8567, https://doi.org/10.3390/su13158567.

Swift, J. A., P. Roberts, N. Boivin, and P. V. Kirch. "Restructuring of Nutrient Flows in Island Ecosystems Following Human Colonization Evidenced by Isotopic Analysis of Commensal Rats." *Proceedings of the National Academy of Sciences* 115 (2018): 6392–6397.

Winter, K. B., K. Chang, and N. K. Lincoln, eds. *Sustainability* 10 (2018). Special issue on Biocultural Restoration in Hawai'i.

Winter, K. B., N. K. Lincoln, F. Berkes, R. Alegado, et al. "Ecomimicry in Indigenous Resource Management: Optimizing Ecosystem Services to Achieve Resource Abundance, with Examples from Hawai'i." *Ecology and Society* 25, 2 (2020): 26.

Contributors

This book is a collaborative work. The lead authors are denoted below with an asterisk (*); one or more of the lead authors cowrote the introduction and each of the chapters in Parts I and III. The coauthors of those chapters and most of the authors and coauthors of chapters in Part II, on individual islands and archipelagoes, are denoted with a dagger (†). Chapter 4, on Rapa Nui, has three coauthors whose main contribution was to the experiment discussed in that chapter; these three are denoted with a double dagger (‡).

Atholl Anderson,† Ngāi Tahu Research Centre, University of Canterbury, New Zealand

Kamanamaikalani Beamer,* Hui ʻĀina Momona Program, Hawaiʻinuiākea School of Hawaiian Knowledge, and Richardson School of Law, all at the University of Hawaiʻi at Mānoa, Honolulu, Hawaiʻi

Elisabeth S. V. Burns,‡ School of World Studies, Virginia Commonwealth University, Richmond, Virginia

Everett Carpenter,‡ Department of Chemistry, Virginia Commonwealth University, Richmond, Virginia

Oliver A. Chadwick,† Department of Geography, University of California, Santa Barbara, California

T. Kaeo Duarte,† Land Assets Division, Kamehameha Schools, Honolulu, Hawaiʻi

Sonia Haoa,† Fundación Matarangi, Rapa Nui, Chile

Caitlin S. M. Hunt,‡ Department of Chemistry, Virginia Commonwealth University, Richmond, Virginia

Patrick V. Kirch,† Department of Anthropology, University of Hawaiʻi at Mānoa, Honolulu, Hawaiʻi

Natalie Kurashima,† Land Assets Division, Kamehameha Schools, Honolulu, Hawaiʻi

Thegn N. Ladefoged,[†] Department of Anthropology, School of Social Sciences, University of Auckland, Auckland, New Zealand

Noa K. Lincoln,[†] Department of Tropical Plant and Soil Sciences, University of Hawai'i at Mānoa, Honolulu, Hawai'i

Pamela A. Matson,[†] Department of Earth System Science, Stanford University, Stanford, California

Christopher M. Stevenson,[†] School of World Studies, Virginia Commonwealth University, Richmond, Virginia

Te Maire Tau,[*] Ngāi Tahu Research Centre, University of Canterbury, Christchurch, New Zealand

Mehana Blaich Vaughan,[†] Department of Natural Resources and Environmental Management, University of Hawai'i at Mānoa, Honolulu, Hawai'i

Peter M. Vitousek,[*] Department of Biology, Stanford University, Stanford, California

Kawika B. Winter,[†] Hawai'i Institute of Marine Biology, University of Hawai'i at Mānoa, Honolulu, Hawai'i

Index

Page numbers followed by "f" indicate a figure.

adaptive radiation, 5–6, 27–28
agriculture: cultivation similarities and differences, 174–175, 181, 192; industrial agriculture, 199; mineral weathering, 91–93; nutrient removal, 82; rainfall and, 76; soil types, 124–125. *See also* Hawai'i; Māori; orchard gardens; Rapa Nui; rock gardens; Tikopia
ahupua'a: definition of, 39, 55; harmony with the past, 39–40; land divisions in, 54–56, 63; Makahiki festival, 60; overseers of, 62; trade among, 61; watershed resource management, 42, 64, 66, 72, 196. *See also* Halele'a *moku*; Kaua'i; Kona *moku*; Ko'olau *moku*; watersheds
"Ahupua'a Poster," 37, 38f, 39, 42, 63, 74
'āina (inhabited land), 36, 40–44, 50, 64, 73–74
akua (gods), 11, 56, 69, 119–120, 186. See also *atua* (Māori gods)
Anda, M., 86
Anderson, Atholl, 133

Aotearoa: ancestors' practices, 175–176; biophysical conditions, 24; climate of, 24–25; Cook and, 12; food storage, 195; fortifications on, 177–178; island names, 111; language, 143, 183; migrating birds and, 16; Polynesians and, 4, 6, 19, 180; rock gardens, 84; trading networks, 176; unique trees of, 183. *See also* New Zealand
aquaculture, 31, 39, 50, 55, 59, 63, 195
arboriculture, 59, 66, 94, 97–98, 109
Armstrong, Karen, 153–154
atua (Māori gods): ancestors and, 186; communication with dead, 161–162, 165; creation tradition, 144; cultural impositions on the land, 172; felling a tree, 166–169; *hau* (winds), 146–148; mountains and, 152; Papatūānuku, 152, 159; question of sacredness, 169; Rata, 166, 168–169; removal of, 165–166; Tāne, 152, 166, 168–169; voices of, 156–158, 163, 165. *See also* Ngāi Tahu
Australia, 13–14

Bali, 13
Banks, Joseph, 170–171
Beamer, Kamanamaikalani, 186
Best, Elsdon, 141–142, 151, 159–160, 172
biodiversity, 181–184
Bork, Hans-Rudolf, 80
Brown, A. A., 128

Campbell, Joseph, 153
Chadwick, Oliver, 192
Chatham Islands, 111, 117, 121, 136
Cook, James, 12, 17–18, 70, 170–171
Crema, Enrico R., 128

Darwin, Charles, 5, 27
deities. See akua; atua
Dillon, Peter, 106

Earle, Augustus, 169, 172
East Polynesia, 112–113, 115–118, 121, 126–127, 171
Ecography, 122
ecomimicry, 192–193
ecosystems, biophysical changes, 23–24
Eliade, Mircia, 153
environmental determinism, 2–3, 159, 177–178, 181
Europeans, 17–19, 61–62, 70, 135, 143, 170

Fiji, 14–15
First Nations' Futures Program, 187
Firth, Raymond, 94, 96, 104, 106–108
food sources and food crops: alga, 47, 54–55; bottle gourd (hue, ipu), 17, 51, 81, 118–119, 124; fish and seaweed, 49, 54–55, 96, 104–105; growing conditions and, 51–53, 59, 65; island similarities, 174–175; ki, the ti plant (Cordyline terminalis), 53, 119, 124; manioc, 98–99; masi pits (crop storage), 105, 109; moa (flightless bird), 115, 122, 129, 137; pigs, 101, 103, 106, 108, 117; poi, 71; pulaka (giant swamp taro), 96–98, 109, 181; sustainability and, 25; sweet potato (kumara, 'uala), 17, 81–82, 118–119, 124, 126–127, 130–131, 138, 180; taro (kalo), 23, 41, 52, 57, 68, 71, 81–82, 96, 99, 119, 124, 181–182, 186; taro paddies (lo'i kalo), 37, 39, 53–54, 59, 66, 69, 175–176, 186–187, 195; wild food resources, 96, 108, 122, 124, 137; yam ('uhi), 81, 97–98, 119, 124. See also agriculture; aquaculture; arboriculture; resource management
forests: deforestation, 77–78, 80, 122, 128, 191; harvesting, 37, 40; impact of Polynesians, 23; planting, 68; tree varieties and names, 183–184; uplands, 51, 53, 63. See also arboriculture

genealogy, 30
The Great Transformation (Armstrong), 153

Hā'ena, 55, 58, 61–62, 71–72
Halele'a moku: agriculture in, 53–54; ahupua'a system, 49, 58–59, 64; community land groups (hui), 71–72; fisheries and, 55; food surplus, 62; geology of, 37, 44, 46–47, 49; Polynesians and, 179; social-environmental systems, 180; trade among ahupua'a, 61; watersheds in, 64, 180

Hāloanakalaukapalili, 41
Hanapēpē, 61
Hannahs, Neil J. Kahoʻokele,
    30, 40
Haoa, Sonia, 192
Hawaiʻi, 45f, 48f; agriculture in, 51,
    59, 65–71, 179, 194–196; ahupuaʻa
    system in, 56, 58–59, 64;
    ʻāina-based practices, 43–44;
    community land groups (hui),
    71–74; discovery of, 16; diversity
    of, 36; environmental impact in,
    177; Europeas and, 61–62, 70;
    genealogy, 41; hierarchical
    system, 55–56, 58, 177–178; kānaka
    maoli (people of this land), 41,
    186; kōʻele system (taxation),
    59–60; land divisions in, 55–56;
    language, 182–183; Māhele (land
    privatization), 57–58, 71;
    methodology, 43–44; plantations,
    70–71; Polynesians and, 30, 40–41,
    46, 178–179; privatization of land,
    71; resource management, 41–42,
    50–51, 66–68, 174–176; rulers of,
    57–58, 60; sustainability and,
    196–197; trade among ahupuaʻa,
    61; traditional land and sea use,
    37–39, 54; two-way voyages, 16
Hawaiʻi State Department of Land
    and Natural Resources, 73
Hensel, Julius, 84
Herewini Ira, 158
Hiʻiakaikapoliopele, 62
A History of Jerusalem (Armstrong),
    153
Hiva (Marquesas Islands), 16, 181
Hōkūleʻa (a double-hulled canoe),
    15
The Holocene (Newnham), 128
Hoʻohōkūkalani, 41, 186
Horrocks, Mark, 80

ʻili, definition of, 56
Indonesia, 14
islands, study of, 27–28, 30–31

Journal of Island and Coastal
    Archaeology, 128
Journal of the Polynesian Society,
    160
Journal of the Royal Society of
    New Zealand, 116

Kamehameha, 58, 60–61
Kamehameha Schools, 71
kānaka (Native Hawaiian), 36–37,
    39
Kanaloa, 11, 69
Kauaʻi, 46–47, 58
Keauhou, 56, 64–65
Kermadec Island, 111, 117, 135
Kirch, Patrick, 6–7, 177–178,
    192–194
Kohala region, 64–65, 67, 195
Kona moku, 52f; agriculture in, 39,
    51–53, 67; ahupuaʻa system in,
    55–57, 59–60, 63–65, 72;
    aquaculture of, 50; Cook and,
    70; geology of, 39, 44, 46–47; lele
    system, 57; Polynesians and, 46,
    179–180; rulers and political
    system, 60–61, 65; salt produc-
    tion, 51; trade among ahupuaʻa,
    61; watersheds in, 64–65, 180
Koʻolau moku: agriculture in,
    53–54; ahupuaʻa system, 58–59;
    exploration of, 44; fisheries and,
    49, 55; fishpond restoration, 73;
    food surplus, 62; forests spared
    by lava flow, 72; geology of,
    46–47, 49; overseers of, 62;
    Polynesians and, 179; watersheds
    in, 37, 64
Kurashima, Natalie, 39, 177

Ladefoged, Thegn N., 81–83, 192
Landscape and Memory (Schama),
    153
language: Austronesian language
    family, 14–15; linguistic
    similarities, 17, 174
Lapita network, 99, 101
Latham, Andrew David MacDuff,
    122
Lincoln, Noa, 39, 177
lo'i kalo (taro paddy), 37, 39, 53–54,
    175–176, 186, 195
Lombok, 13
Lopes, O. M. M., 86
Lorrey, Andrew, 130
Louwagie, Grant, 82

Mahinga kai nō Tonganui
    (New Zealand). *See* Aotearoa
Ma'ilikūkahi, 56
Makahiki festival, 60–61
Malo, David, 44
Manōkalanipō, 58
Māori: agriculture of, 124, 137;
    demography of, 126–129; food
    traditions, 112, 118, 176; genealo-
    gies and ancestors, 146, 148–151,
    159; migration north to south,
    132–133, 135, 141; mind and spirit
    location (*hinengaro*), 160,
    163–165, 171–172; outward or
    return migration, 116; *pā*,
    hidden knowledge and mind,
    142–143, 148, 151, 159–160;
    pu-kanohi (lagoons), 143; status
    relationships, 120–121; technol-
    ogy and, 169–170; tribal elders,
    142, 147, 152, 158, 187; warfare and
    Tū, 131–132, 161, 163. See also
    atua; New Zealand; Ngāi Tahu
*Maori-Polynesian Comparative
    Dictionary* (Tregear), 164

Martin, William, 121
Matson, Pamela, 185, 187
Maui (character), 12
Mauna Kea, 61
McRae, Jane, 147
Melanesians, 19–21
Micronesians, 19–21
Mieth, Andreas, 80
migrations: to the Americas, 17;
    into East Polynesia, 115; to
    Hawaiian Archipelago and
    Aotearoa, 16; into Island
    Southeast Asia, 14; into Remote
    Oceania, 14–16; into Southeast
    Asia (Australia), 13; into South
    Polynesia, 112–113, 115–116
Miscellaneous Manuscripts
    (White), 169
missionaries, 62, 70, 107, 109
model systems, 26–27
moku: definition of, 37, 55; in
    Hawai'i, 57–58; resource
    management in, 42, 63, 176. *See
    also* Halele'a *moku*; Kona *moku*;
    Ko'olau *moku*
*Monuments and People in the
    Pacific* (Anderson), 133

Nāpali: Makahiki festival, 60–61;
    trade, 61
*Narrative of the Fighting on the
    East Coast* (Nihoniho), 161
navigation: celestial, 15, 18–19;
    migratory birds and, 16
New Guinea, 13–14
Newnham, Rewi, 128
New Zealand, 114f, 123f, 134f;
    climate change effect, 129–131,
    135–137; deforestation, 122, 125;
    geography of, 115, 122; horticul-
    ture and crop cultivation,
    118–119, 125, 130–131; land

divisions in, 121, 137; outlying
islands of, 135–136; resource
management, 176; soil types,
124–125; South Island, 151–152;
subsistence and exchange,
137–138; two islands as fish head
and tail, 120. *See also* Aotearoa;
Māori
Ngāi Tahu: *atua* (gods), 147–148,
152–153, 156, 158–159, 161–163,
165–166, 168, 172, 186; genealogies and ancestors, 151–153; land
divisions in, 120; mountains
and, 151, 154–155, 158; move to
South Island, 133, 179; success of
trade, 137–138; traditions and
rituals of, 144–146
Nihoniho, Matutaera (Tuta), 151,
161–163
Niue, 120
Norfolk Island, 111, 117, 136
Nunes, J. M. G., 86

ʻōiwi (Native Hawaiian), 37
orchard gardens, 94, 96–99, 102,
105, 109

Papahānaumokuākea, 41, 186
Pāpāhia, 154
Polynesia and Polynesians, 20f;
colonization evidence, 117–118;
East and South comparison, 113,
115, 119, 126; European classification, 19–20; family and, 187;
island study, 28–30; mind and
spirit location, 171; navigators,
15–17; origins of, 11–13, 19, 21;
Polynesian Triangle, 4, 19, 20f;
status relationships, 120; sustainability and, 185–186, 188–189,
189f, 190, 190f, 196–198;
traditions and rituals of, 171. *See*

also East Polynesia; migrations;
South Polynesia
Polynesian Triangle, 19f–20f
Polynesian Voyaging Society,
15–16
Puhi-rawaho, 156

Quaternary International, 130

Ramos, Claudete Gindri, 85. *See
also* watersheds
Rapa Nui (Easter Island), 77f;
agriculture in, 78, 81–82, 85;
archaeology of, 80–81; ceremonial architecture, 177–178;
colonization, 192; deforestation,
77–78, 80, 191; food surplus,
90–91; geology of, 76, 79,
83; rainfall, 76; resources
collapse, 77, 190. *See also* rock
gardens
Rawiri Te Maire, 150
resource management, 41–42,
50–51, 66–68, 176
rock gardens, 79f; environmental
adaptation, 81, 191; European
contact and, 78; minerals and
nutrient levels, 80, 82–86,
91–93; minerals experiment,
87–90
Rongo, 119–120

The Sacred and Profane (Eliade),
153
sacred geography, 153–155
sailing conditions and vessels:
spritsails, 116–117, 133; wind
directions, 117
Salmond, Anne, 141
Samoa, 14–15, 105, 164
Schama, Simon, 153
Sherwood, Sarah C., 80, 92

social-environmental systems:
ancestors' practices, 41–43, 175;
biophysical conditions, 199;
environmental influence, 2, 35;
food gathering and agriculture,
31; kinship of plants, animals,
and land, 36; local conditions
and sustainability, 24–25;
Polynesian opportunities, 6–8,
28, 30; similarities of, 173–174;
sustainability and, 185, 194, 197;
traditional practices, 70,
176–180; understanding, 3, 5;
water and watersheds, 63–64;
zero population growth and, 109
Society Islands, 111
South Polynesia: colonization of,
127; crop cultivation, 118, 129;
depletion of natural resources,
112; geography of, 113, 115;
maritime mobility, 119;
migrations, 116–117; status
relationships, 121; unique rituals
of, 136
"Spiritual Concepts of the Maori"
(Best), 160
Stevenson, Christopher, 192
Subantarctic Islands, 111
sustainability: definition of, 185;
genealogy and, 187; in Hawai'i,
176; models of, 30, 190, 199;
natural capital and, 194;
overcoming challenges of, 25, 31;
in Polynesia, 8; social capital
and, 196; study of, 5, 188, 197; in
Tikopia, 7, 106, 109
Swift, J. A., 194

Tau, Te Maire, 188
Te Rangikaheke, 146
"Three Islands and an
Archipelago" (Kirch), 6

Tikopia, 95f, 100f; agriculture in,
98, 104, 177–178, 181, 193;
agroecosystem, 101–103, 192–194;
archaeology of, 99–101;
demography of, 94, 108; forest
clearance, 103; geology of, 95–96,
102, 104; long-distance exchange
network, 103; *masi* pits (crop
storage), 105, 109; pigs and
removal of, 101, 103, 106, 108;
Polynesian speakers in, 104;
Rakisu zone, 98–99, 102–103;
Sinapupu Phase, 99, 102–104;
Tuakamali Phase, 100, 104–106;
zero population growth, 107,
109. See also orchard gardens
Tiramōrehu, Matiaha, 144, 146, 148,
152, 169
Tonga, 14–15, 105, 127
Tregear, Edward, 164
Tupaia of Raiatea, 170–171

'Umialiloa, 56

Vaughan, Mehana Blaich, 37, 177
Vitousek, Peter, 83, 187
The Voyage of the Beagle (Darwin),
5, 27
*A Voyage Towards the South Pole
and Round the World* (Cook),
12, 17

Wailua *moku*, 58
Waipā Foundation, 37, 71
Wākea, 41, 186
Wallace's Line, 13
Waruwarutu, 148
watersheds, 10, 39, 42, 58, 63–66
White, John, 169
Winter, Kawika, 175, 182, 192, 196
Wi Pokuku, 148, 150
Wozniak, Joan A., 80

CPSIA information can be obtained
at www.ICGtesting.com
Printed in the USA
JSHW020035240123
36615JS00001B/3

9 780300 253009

Kakalak, North Carolina Winning Poems (North Carolina Poetry Society), *Bay Leaves,* and other journals and anthologies.

Ellen Summers leads writing workshops in the Amherst Writers and Artists method and teaches writing at the Servant Leadership School in Greensboro. She holds a doctorate in English from The University of North Carolina at Chapel Hill and taught writing and literature at the college level for twenty years. Her poems have appeared in *Wittenberg Review* and *Hiram Poetry Review.* She serves as facilitator of the Novel Writers critique group.

Don Webb is from Virginia and has lived in Greensboro for sixteen years. He started his writing career in 1984 with school publications, and is also a professional musician, having arranged and written music since 1992. He lives in Greensboro with his daughter Maddie, a source of great inspiration.

Stephen G. Wessells, a native of Richmond, Virginia, attended Guilford College and moved to Greensboro in 1975. He has written poetry for over forty years, and is dedicated to restoring formalism to respectability. Major influences include Ezra Pound and the Romantic poets.

Susan Dean Wessells wrote her first poem for a school play when she was eight years old. At fourteen, she picked up her pen again and has been writing poetry ever since. Her life has been rich with varied experiences that nourish her writing. In 2007 she realized a lifelong dream when she was a contestant on the *Jeopardy!* game show. She is currently working on a novel about vampire nuns.

CPSIA information can be obtained at www.ICGtesting.com
Printed in the USA
BVOW012325080112

280014BV00001B/5/P

9 780984 934904